GCSE AQA Additional
Applied Science
The Workbook

This book is for anyone doing **GCSE AQA Additional Applied Science**.

GCSE Science is all about **understanding how science works**.
And not only that — understanding it well enough to be able to question
what you hear on TV and read in the papers.

But you can't do that without a fair chunk of **background knowledge**. Hmm, tricky.

This book is full of **tricky questions**... each one designed to make you **sweat**
— because that's the only way you'll get any **better**.

There are questions to see **what facts** you know. There are questions to see how
well you can **apply those facts**. And there are questions to see how well you
understand the role of **scientists** in the **real world**.

It's also got some daft bits in to try and make the whole
experience at least vaguely entertaining for you.

What CGP is all about

Our sole aim here at CGP is to produce the highest
quality books — carefully written, immaculately presented
and dangerously close to being funny.

Then we work our socks off to get them out to you — at the cheapest possible prices.

Contents

Published by CGP

Editors:
Mary Falkner, Helen Ronan, Camilla Simson, Megan Tyler.

Contributors:
Mark Edwards, Max Fishel, Paddy Gannon, Anne Hetherington,
Adrian Schmit, Sophie Watkins, Chris Workman.

ISBN: 978 1 84762 885 5

With thanks to Barrie Crowther, Helena Hayes, Rosie McCurrie and Philip Rushworth
for the proofreading.

With thanks to Anna Lupton for the copyright research.

Pages 2 and 4 contain public sector information published by the Health and Safety Executive
and licensed under the Open Government Licence v1.0.

KITEMARK and the Kitemark device are reproduced on pages 28 and 44 with kind permission
of The British Standards Institution. They are registered trademarks in the United Kingdom
and in certain other countries.

Groovy website: www.cgpbooks.co.uk

Printed by Elanders Ltd, Newcastle upon Tyne.
Jolly bits of clipart from CorelDRAW®
Based on the classic CGP style created by Richard Parsons.

Following Standard Procedures

Q1   It's important that scientists understand **standard procedures**.

a)   Which of the statements below describes what a **standard procedure** is? **Circle** the correct answer.

A set of laws that tell scientists how to write their reports.

The equipment that scientists have to use.

Clear instructions that describe how to do an experiment.

b)   **Why** is it important that scientists use **standard procedures**?
Tick the box next to the correct answer.

☐   It stops other scientists copying their work.

☐   It helps to keep results consistent.

☐   It saves time because scientists don't have to complete a risk assessment.

☐   It makes the work more exciting for the scientists.

Q2   Sammy is carrying out an experiment using a **standard procedure**.

a)   **Circle** the **six** steps below that are part of a standard procedure.

Complete a risk assessment.

Get all your equipment ready and set up your working area.

Decide how you are going to carry out your investigation.

Make changes to the instructions as you go along.

Follow the instructions one step at a time.

Select instruments with an appropriate sensitivity.

Do your experiment as quickly as possible.

Look for anomalous results and repeat your measurements if necessary.

Read the procedure — make sure you understand everything.

b)   Sammy wants to let **other scientists** know about her results.
Explain how Sammy could do this.

....

....

Top Tips: So, there you go. A lovely page of questions all about standard procedures.
But they're not just for show... It's really important that all scientists **use** and **understand** standard
procedures — that includes **you** when you're doing experiments. Have a go at these questions and
you'll soon get your head around what a standard procedure is and how to use one. Enjoy.

**Avoiding Hazards**

Q1   Draw lines to match the **symbols** below with their **meanings** and **hazards**.

a) | toxic | | can cause death if swallowed, inhaled or absorbed through the skin |

b) | biohazard | | can explode |

c) | highly flammable | | provides oxygen which allows other materials to burn more fiercely |

d) | explosive | | contains biological material that could be harmful |

e) | harmful | | like toxic, but not quite as dangerous |

f) | oxidising | | catches fire easily |

Q2   Reece has splashed acid in his eye and needs an **emergency eye wash**.

a)   Tick the box next to the **safe condition sign** he should look for in the lab.

b)   Reece wants to put up a **mandatory sign** to stop other people splashing acid in their eyes. Explain what a mandatory sign is.

....

Q3   There are four common types of **fire extinguisher**: water, carbon dioxide, foam and dry powder. Tick the boxes to show the fire extinguishers that could be used to put out each type of fire.

	water	carbon dioxide	foam	dry powder
a) A pile of text books that's on fire.	☐	☐	☐	☐
b) A computer that has caught fire.	☐	☐	☐	☐
c) An unknown liquid chemical that's on fire.	☐	☐	☐	☐

<u>Health and Safety</u>

Q1   Complete the sentences by choosing the correct phrases from the box below.

The 1946 Ruling on Health and Safety at Work	Health and Safety Executive
Health and Safety at Work Act (1974)	Health and Safety Bureau of Investigations

a) The .... is a set of laws that deals with health and safety in the workplace.

b) The .... checks that the laws that deal with health and safety in the workplace are being followed.

Q2   It's very important to carry out a **risk assessment** when you're planning an experiment.

a) Complete the passage using words from the box below.

harmed	reduce	hazards	harm	action

A risk assessment should identify any stage in the process that could cause ....
This usually involves identifying .... and the people who might be
.... Risk assessments also include what .... can be taken
to .... the risk.

b) A scientist has identified **three risks** for his acid-base titration experiment.
Complete the table by giving an example of how he could **reduce each risk**.

Risk	How to Reduce Risk
Cuts from broken glass.	
Skin irritation from contact with alkali.	
Eye damage from acid splash.	

Q3   Emily is doing a **health and safety check** of a work station in the school lab.
She's not sure what to check. Give **three** things that Emily should check.

1. ....

2. ....

3. ....

<u>Mixed Questions for Section 1</u>

Q1   Circle **five hazards** around Tatania's work station.

Q2   Milly has been given a **standard procedure** to follow for her experiment.

a)   She sees the symbol below on a bottle of ammonia she is using.

What does this symbol mean?

....

b)   In the standard procedure, Milly is told that she needs to measure out 25 ml of ammonia.

i)   Circle the measuring equipment she should use.

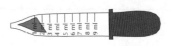   

ii) Explain why Milly should use the piece of measuring equipment you circled in part **i)**.

....

....

c)   Milly measures the amount of hydrochloric acid (HCl) needed to neutralise the ammonia. Her results are given in the table below.

Measurement	Volume of HCl (ml)
1	51
2	50
3	36
4	51

Circle the anomalous result.

Section 1 — Working Safely in Science

Healthcare Scientists

Q1 Which of the following things does a **pharmacist** do?
Tick the box next to the correct answer.

Helps people with eating disorders. ☐

Helps patients get as much benefit as they can from the drugs they are taking. ☐

Helps people understand what they need to eat to stay healthy. ☐

Q2 Tom is training for a marathon. He goes to see a **nutritionist**.
Complete the passage below using the words from the box.

healthy	athletes	food	balanced diet

Nutritionists give people information on .... and nutrition.

They help people understand what they need to eat to have a ....

and generally stay .... They also work with ....

and suggest diets that could help them do better at their sport.

Q3 Rachael, Henry and Bex all have health problems.
Complete the table below by ticking the box underneath the healthcare scientist who would be most able to **help with their problem**. The first one has been done for you.

Patient and Problem	Healthcare Scientist		
	Pharmacist	Dietician	Physiotherapist
Rachael — An eating disorder		✓	
Henry — A broken leg			
Bex — A heart problem that requires regular medication			

Q4 There are lots of different types of **fitness practitioners**.
Draw a line to match the type of fitness practitioner with the job that they do.

Coach

Sports physiologist

Fitness Trainer

Supervises exercise programmes in gyms and leisure clubs and provides personal training.

Helps athletes improve their physical fitness and strength.

Provides technical training for particular sports or events, as well as general fitness training.

The Blood and Blood Vessels

Q1 **Blood** is mostly made up of four different parts — red blood cells, white blood cells, platelets and plasma. Draw lines to match each part of the blood with the job that it does.

Platelets

Plasma

White blood cells

Red blood cells

Transport oxygen from the lungs to all the cells in the body.

Help the blood to clot at the site of a wound.

Help fight infection.

The liquid that carries everything in the blood.

Q2 Fill in the gaps in the passage about **veins** using words from the box.

valves	thinner	lumen	to	lower

Veins have .... walls than arteries because they transport blood at

.... pressure. Veins transport blood .... the heart.

They have .... to stop the blood flowing the wrong way and

they have a bigger .... than arteries to help the blood flow.

Q3 Huang has fallen off his bike and has a **cut** that won't stop **bleeding**. At the hospital, the doctor tells Huang he has injured an artery.

a) Circle the correct words in each pair to complete the sentences below.

Arteries carry blood **away from** / **to** the heart.

Arteries carry blood at **high** / **low** pressure.

The walls of arteries are strong and **rigid** / **elastic**.

b) If you lightly press an artery, what do you feel each time the heart beats?

....

c) Huang also has bruises on his knees where **capillaries** have been broken. Describe the **function** of the capillaries in the body.

....

....

The Heart

Q1 Padma has been told that she has a high risk of developing **heart disease**.

Her cardiologist explains that heart disease is caused by a build-up of fatty substances in the arteries that supply the heart. This restricts the blood flow to the heart and can cause damage.

a) i) Label the diagram of the heart below, using words from the box.

| right atrium | left ventricle | right ventricle | left atrium |

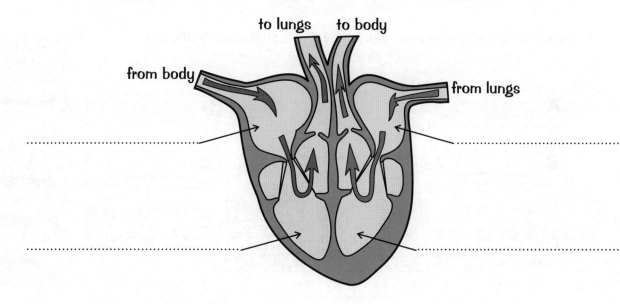

ii) Circle **two valves** on the diagram.

b) The statements below describe the flow of blood **from the body** through the heart and lungs. Number the boxes to put the statements in the correct order. The first one has been done for you.

☐ Blood passes into the left ventricle, which pumps it out and round the whole body.

☐ Blood flows through a valve into the right ventricle.

☐ Blood leaves the heart and flows to the lungs.

[1] Deoxygenated blood from the body enters the right atrium.

☐ Oxygenated blood from the lungs flows into the left atrium.

8

The Lungs and Breathing

Q1 Paul competes in the 400 m relay but has recently noticed he's getting out of breath quicker than usual. His **physiologist** thinks he may have an infection in his lungs.

a) Put the structures of the lungs into the order that air passes through them when **breathing in**.

| A alveoli | B bronchioles | C bronchi | D trachea |

Order: ....

b) In which structure(s) is **carbon dioxide** in the blood exchanged for **oxygen** from the air? Circle the correct answer.

trachea   bronchi   alveoli

c) Label the diagram of the **respiratory system** using the words in the box.

A ....

B ....

C ....

D ....

E ....

F ....

rib

bronchus

trachea

diaphragm

bronchiole

alveoli

Q2 Lester swims for his school **swimming club**. His **coach** makes the team practise **breathing techniques** to improve their performance.

The statements below describe what happens when you **breathe in** and when you **breathe out**. Number the boxes (1-6) to put each set of sentences in order. The first one in each set has been done for you.

Breathing IN

[ ] The chest cavity gets larger.

[1] The intercostal muscles contract.

[ ] The diaphragm contracts and flattens out.

[ ] Air is drawn in.

[ ] The ribcage is pulled up and out.

[ ] The pressure inside the lungs decreases.

Breathing OUT

[ ] Air is forced out.

[ ] The chest cavity gets smaller.

[1] The intercostal muscles relax.

[ ] The pressure inside the lungs increases.

[ ] The ribcage drops in and down.

[ ] The diaphragm relaxes and arches up.

Top Tips: Knowing the order of what goes on when you breathe in and out is tricky. But if you get a bit stuck, you've got a working model right in front of you to help you out. Just take a deep breath — you should see your lungs go up and out. This gives you a bit of a clue to what's happening...

Section 2 — Health, Exercise and Nutrition

Measuring Lung Capacity and Breathing Rate

Q1   Michael is a professional swimmer. He is trying to improve his performance for a big competition that's coming up, so he goes to see a **sports physiologist**.

a)   Circle the piece of **equipment** the sports physiologist would use to test Michael's **lung capacity**.

spirometer   stethoscope   microscope

b)   The sports physiologist tested Michael's **tidal volume** and **vital capacity**. Draw lines to join each term to its correct meaning.

Tidal volume   The most air you can possibly breathe in or out in one breath.

Vital capacity   The amount you breath in (or out) with each breath.

c)   i)   Briefly describe how the sports physiologist would measure Michael's **vital capacity**.

....

....

....

ii)   The sports physiologist took three measurements of Michael's **tidal volume** and then found the average. Explain why she did this.

....

d)   The sports physiologist was interested in how Michael's **breathing rate** and **tidal volume** changed when he exercised.

i)   Circle the correct word in each pair to complete the sentences below.

> The number of breaths you take every **minute / second** is known as your breathing rate.
>
> During exercise your breathing rate **increases / decreases**.
>
> Your tidal volume increases, meaning that you take **shallower / deeper** breaths.

ii)   Michael took 160 breaths in four minutes. What is his breathing rate?

....

Top Tips: Tidal volume is like, well, the tides in the sea: in and out, in and out, in and out... When you exercise, tidal volume increases, helping you to take in oxygen and push out carbon dioxide.

Section 2 — Health, Exercise and Nutrition

Respiration and Exercise

Q1 Matteo is trying to improve his overall fitness. His fitness trainer designs a programme for him. The training exercises in his programme are classed as 'aerobic' or 'anaerobic', depending on which kind of **respiration** is mostly used.

a) Tick the correct boxes to show whether the statements are **true** or **false**.

	True	False
Respiration releases energy.	☐	☐
Respiration uses glucose.	☐	☐
Energy from respiration is used to make your muscles contract.	☐	☐
Respiration always requires oxygen.	☐	☐
The heart and lungs allow glucose and carbon dioxide to be transported to the muscles for respiration.	☐	☐

b) i) Complete the word equation for **aerobic** respiration.

.... + Oxygen ⟶ .... + Water (+ Energy)

ii) Write the formula equation for **aerobic** respiration.

.... + ... ⟶ .... + ... (+ Energy)

c) Write the word equation for **anaerobic** respiration.

....

d) Circle the correct words in each pair to complete the sentences below.

i) Anaerobic respiration happens when there's not enough **carbon dioxide / oxygen** available.

ii) Aerobic / Anaerobic respiration is the most efficient way to release energy from glucose.

iii) In anaerobic respiration, the break down of glucose is **complete / incomplete**.

e) One of Matteo's training exercises involves doing a series of short sprints. After completing this exercise, Matteo has built up an **oxygen debt**. Complete this passage about oxygen debt using the words from the box.

heart rate	painful	glucose	stop	anaerobically	oxygen

When you respire ...., lactic acid builds up in the muscles, which can be

.... When you .... exercising you'll have an oxygen

debt — your muscles are still short of .... because they haven't been

getting enough for a while. You'll need extra oxygen to convert all the lactic acid that's built

up in your muscles back into .... This means you have to keep breathing

hard and your .... has to stay high for a while to repay the debt.

Higher only

Higher only

Measuring Heart Rate and Recovery

Q1   Yvonne's **coach** wanted to assess her fitness by monitoring her **heart rate** and **breathing rate** before and after a period of **intensive exercise**.

a) Yvonne's coach wants to know what Yvonne's **resting heart rate** is. How would she **measure** this? Circle the correct answer.

Place her thumb on Yvonne's elbow.

Place her hand on Yvonne's forehead.

Place two fingers on Yvonne's wrist.

b) Yvonne's average resting heart rate was 67 beats/min.
After she had exercised her heart rate was 120 beats/min.
Circle the correct words in each pair to complete the sentences below.

> During exercise, Yvonne's muscles contract **more often** / **less often**, so they need more energy.
>
> This energy comes from an increased rate of **sweating** / **respiration**. This means that more
>
> **carbon dioxide** / **oxygen** needs to be delivered to her muscles, so Yvonne's heart rate increases.

c) What other physiological changes occur during exercise? Circle **two** correct answers.

Breathing rate increases.

The volume of blood pumped each heartbeat increases.

Tidal volume decreases.

Sweating decreases.

Think about what happens to you when you exercise.

d) Your **recovery time** is the time it takes your body to get back to normal after exercise. Describe an experiment that Yvonne and her coach could do to measure her **recovery time**.

....

....

....

e) The graph below shows how Yvonne's heart rate changed during one of her training sessions.

i) Draw a cross on the graph to show when Yvonne **stopped** exercising.

ii) Use the graph to work out Yvonne's **recovery time**.

....

....

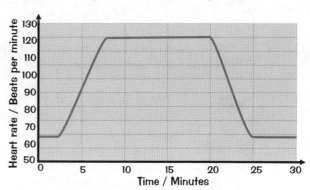

Top Tips: If you're asked to calculate recovery time from a graph in the exam, you just need to look at the time that the person stops exercising and then work out how long it takes for their heart rate to return to the resting level (the same as before exercise began). Nothing too tricky there.

Body Temperature

Q1   Andrew plays **squash** professionally. When Andrew plays he always gets **very hot** and **sweaty**.
A **sports physiologist** thinks Andrew's body is **not very good** at **controlling** his temperature.

a)   Which organ of the body **monitors** and **controls** Andrew's body temperature?

....

b)   The sports physiologist explains to Andrew that his body's thermostat isn't working properly.
What is the correct name for the body's 'thermostat'? Circle the correct answer.

the thermostat centre   the thermoregulatory centre   the pancreas

c)   Body temperature is measured using a **thermometer**.
Draw lines to match each type of thermometer with its description.

An electronic digital thermometer

A thermometer that gives a digital
reading when you put it in your ear.

A clinical thermometer

A plastic strip that's placed on the skin and
changes colour to show the temperature.

A liquid crystal thermometer

A standard thermometer that you
stick under your armpit or tongue.

d)   When Andrew gets too hot, the blood vessels supplying his skin capillaries dilate and he sweats.
Tick the boxes to show whether these statements are **true** or **false**.

True   False

i)   When sweat evaporates, it transfers heat to the environment.   ☐   ☐

ii) Less heat is lost to the surroundings when the blood vessels
supplying the skin capillaries dilate.   ☐   ☐

iii) Sweating causes your body to retain heat.   ☐   ☐

Q2   A rescue team discovered an injured climber on a mountain ledge.
The rescue team were concerned that the mountaineer had a very **low body temperature**.

When you are cold, your blood vessels change in order to help maintain body
temperature. Circle the correct words in the passage below to describe how.

When you're cold, the blood vessels that supply your skin capillaries

dilate / constrict. This means that **more / less** blood gets to the surface of the skin.

This stops the blood from **losing heat to / gaining heat from** the surroundings.

Section 2 — Health, Exercise and Nutrition

Controlling Water

Q1 The body needs to balance **water coming in** against **water going out**.

a) Why do we need to drink **water** when we exercise? Fill in the gap to complete the sentence below.

> To replace the water lost through ....

b) Water is lost from the body in urine. Which **organ** produces urine? Circle the correct answer.

the liver   the pancreas   the kidneys   the stomach

Q2 **Sports scientists** were studying the effect of **water intake** on **urine production**. Groups of people drank a set amount of water during **24 hours**. The amount of **urine** they produced from 12 hours after the beginning of the experiment until 12 hours after the last drink, was monitored.

The results are shown in the graph.

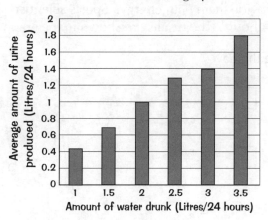

a) Tick the box next to the sentence that describes the **relationship** between the amount of water drunk and the amount of urine produced.

☐ The more water a person drinks the more urine they produce.

☐ The more water a person drinks the less urine they produce.

☐ The amount of water a person drinks has no effect on the amount of urine they produce.

b) i) Who would have the **darker urine**? Circle the correct answer.

The people who drank 1 litre of water.   The people who drank 3 litres of water.

ii) Explain your answer to part **b) i)**.

....

c) The scientists made sure that all the people doing the test ate **exactly** the same food during the test. Tick **one** reason why they did this.

☐ Food contains water.

☐ Eating makes you breathe less.

☐ Food makes you sweat less.

d) Circle the correct word from the pair to complete the following sentence.

To make it a fair test the people taking part in the experiment were not allowed to **read / exercise**.

Controlling Glucose

Q1 Controlling **blood glucose levels** is really important, especially during exercise when the body needs sugar to provide **energy** for the working muscles.

a) Draw lines to match the **organs** with their role in the control of blood glucose levels.

| Liver | The organ that produces insulin. |
| Pancreas | The organ that stores glycogen. |

b) Circle the correct word in each pair to complete the sentences below.

> If circulating blood glucose levels get too **high** / **low** insulin is released.
>
> Insulin stimulates the liver to take up glucose from the blood and store
>
> it as an insoluble carbohydrate called **urea** / **glycogen**.

Q2 Athletes need a constant supply of **glucose** to provide them with **energy**. **Sports scientists** studied the **level of glucose** in an athlete's blood over 24 hours. The results are shown in the graph.

a) i) The athlete did one session of training during the day. When do you think they **trained**?

Write **A**, **B**, **C**, **D** or **E** in the following box. ☐

ii) When do you think the athlete had **breakfast**?

Write **A**, **B**, **C**, **D** or **E** in the following box. ☐

iii) Explain your answer to part **a) ii)**.

....

....

b) If the level of insulin in the athlete's blood was plotted, which of the following **patterns** would you expect it to show? Tick the correct answer.

☐ A similar pattern to the blood glucose.

☐ The inverse of the blood glucose (i.e. trends go in opposite directions to blood glucose).

☐ A constant level throughout the day.

Higher only

c) The next morning the athlete skips breakfast and does two training sessions before 11 am. What **hormone** do you think the athlete's pancreas will be producing by late morning? Explain your answer.

....

....

....

Section 2 — Health, Exercise and Nutrition

Measuring Glucose and Muscle Strength

Q1 Magnus is a **hammer thrower**. His coach wants to measure his **forearm strength**.

Number the boxes (1 to 4) to put the instructions into the right order for measuring strength using a **handgrip dynamometer**. The first one has been done for you.

☐ Record the best reading.

☐ Repeat three times.

[1] Hold the dynamometer in your dominant hand and adjust it to match your hand size.

☐ With your elbow at a right angle to your body, grip the dynamometer as hard as you can.

Q2 **Diabetes** is a disease where the body doesn't produce enough insulin. People with diabetes have to carefully **monitor** their **blood glucose level**.

a) A **glucose test strip** or a **digital meter** can be used to test blood glucose levels. Which is more **accurate**? Circle the correct answer.

Glucose test strip   Digital meter

b) Glucose in your **urine** can be a symptom of diabetes. Describe how you would **test** for glucose in urine.

....

....

Q3 Kieran is a professional **football player**. He also has **diabetes**. He tries to keep his **blood glucose level** in the same range as people who don't have diabetes.

Kieran **tested** his blood before a game using a **glucose test strip**. Complete these instructions describing how to use a glucose test strip using the words from the box.

colour	blood	glucose	sterile	insulin

Instructions

1. Prick your finger using a special .... 'pen'.

2. Put a drop of .... onto the glucose test strip.

3. Compare it to the manufacturer's .... chart.

4. The strip turns a different colour depending on how much .... is present.

5. Use this result to work out how much .... to inject.

Bones, Muscles and Joints

Q1   **Physiotherapists** need a good knowledge of the body's **bones** and **muscles** to do their job.

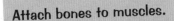

a)   Name **one** job that the skeleton does.

....

b)   Draw lines to match the following structures to their correct description.

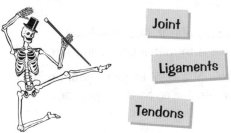

Joint

Ligaments

Tendons

Attach bones to muscles.

The point where two or more bones meet.

Hold bones together.

Q2   The diagram below is of a human **arm**.

a)   Name the structures **A-E** on the diagram using the words in the box.

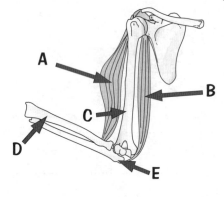

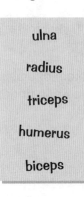

ulna

radius

triceps

humerus

biceps

A ....

B ....

C ....

D ....

E ....

b)   Name the part of the arm that acts as a **pivot**.

....

c)   Give the letter of the muscle that is **contracted** in the diagram.   ....

d)   Give the letter of the muscle that is **relaxed** in the diagram.   ....

e)   What name is given to **muscles** that work in **pairs**? ....

Higher only

Q3   The diagram below shows a **synovial joint**.

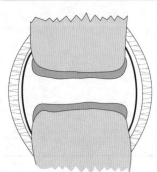

a)   i)   Draw an arrow on the diagram pointing to the **synovial membrane**.

ii)   The synovial membrane produces **synovial fluid**.
What is the **function** of the synovial fluid?

....

b)   The ends of bones at a synovial joint are covered with **cartilage**.
What is the **function** of the cartilage?

....

Joints and Forces

Q1   **Fitness practitioners** help athletes to improve their **performance** using **biomechanics** — the study of the **forces** that act on the body.

a)   Complete the passage below using the words from the box.

pivot	perpendicular	moment	multiplying

When a force acts on something which has a .... , it creates a turning or twisting force. A turning or twisting force is also called a .... It can be found by ...., the force by the .... distance.

b)   What **units** are moments measured in? Circle the correct answer.

N (newtons)   **Nm (newton metres)**   **m (metres)**

Q2   Andy is a physiotherapist. One of his patients has an arm injury. Andy gets the patient to hold a **weight** to increase the **strength** of their **injured arm**, as shown in the diagram below.

a)   Andy is trying to calculate the **moment of the weight** acting on the injured arm.

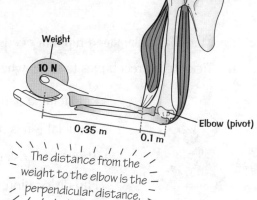

Weight

10 N

0.35 m   0.1 m

Elbow (pivot)

i)   How **far away** is the weight from the pivot (elbow)?

....

ii) Calculate the **moment** acting on the weight.

....

....

....

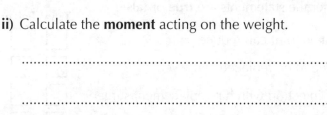

The distance from the weight to the elbow is the perpendicular distance.

b)   For the arm to stay **still**, the **moment** of the **muscle** has to be the **same** as the moment of the **weight**. Circle the correct words in each pair to complete the sentences below.

i)   If the muscle had a bigger moment than the weight, the arm would **lift up / move down**.

ii) If the weight had a bigger moment than the muscle, the arm would **lift up / move down**.

c)   Andy wants to know the **force** that the **muscle** is applying to keep the **arm still** when holding the weight. Use your answer to **Q2 a) ii)** to calculate the force applied by the muscle.

....

....

Top Tips: Moments might seem a bit physic-sy and math-sy (urgh), but don't panic. Once you've got what the question is asking you it's just a case of plugging the numbers into the equation.

Injuries and Artificial Joints

Q1 Debbie **has injured** her leg while out running, so she is going to see a **sports physiotherapist**.

a) The table below shows information about some common **skeletal-muscular injuries**.
Use the words below the table to complete the missing information from the table.

Skeletal-muscular injury	Description	Usual cause
....	Stretched or torn ligament	Violent twisting
Torn muscle	Muscle tears	....
Ruptured tendon	....	Over-stretching
....	Bone comes out of normal position	Twisting
Fractured bone	Bone breaks	....
Torn cartilage	....	Sudden impact

Dislocation   Too much stress   Sudden over-stretching

Tendon breaks   Ligament damage   Cartilage tears

b) Name **one** way that a sports physiotherapist might **treat** a patient
with a skeletal-muscular injury like Debbie.

....

Q2 Mary has a **damaged hip** that needs to be replaced with an **artificial joint**.

a) Tick the correct boxes to show whether the statements are **true** or **false**.

	True	False
Replacing a damaged joint can reduce pain.	☐	☐
Artificial joints need to be replaced every year.	☐	☐
There is no risk of infection with hip replacement surgery.	☐	☐
Hip dislocation is more common with artificial joints.	☐	☐

b) The **material** used to make an **artificial joint** has to be chosen **carefully**.

i) What **properties** should the material used to make an artificial joint have?
Circle the **three** correct words from the box below.

heavy   smooth   durable   reactive   rough   lightweight

ii) Mary's twin sister Sylvia needs a **knee replacement**.
Circle the correct words in each pair to complete the sentences below.

Mary's replacement hip joint will **require a lot of movement / carry a lot of weight**.

The material used for Mary's artificial hip joint needs to be both strong and

sturdy / flexible, so **titanium / plastic** is ideal. Sylvia's replacement knee joint will

require a lot of movement / carry a lot of weight. The material used for this must be

strong and **sturdy / flexible** so the best material to use would be **titanium / plastic**.

Section 2 — Health, Exercise and Nutrition

Energy Needs

Q1 Laura is in a **hockey team** and is visiting a **dietician** to find out how much she should eat to stay at a **healthy weight**.

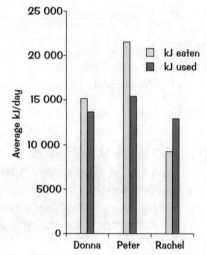

a) Complete the passage below using the words in the box.

fat	eat	lose	gain

People should balance the number of kJ they .... (their 'intake') with the number of kJ they use up during activity. If their intake is greater than their use, they'll .... weight. If their intake is less than their use, they will .... weight. Weight gain is caused by the extra energy being stored as ....

b) The graph shows the average number of kilojoules (kJ) eaten and used per day by some of Laura's team mates. The average was calculated over a period of one month.

  i) Which person is most likely to lose weight?

  ....

  ii) Which person is most likely to gain weight?

  ....

Q2 The food you eat provides you with **energy**.
Different people need different amounts of energy each day.

a) This is the formula for calculating a person's **basic energy requirement**:

Basic energy requirement (kJ/day) = 5.4 × 24 × body mass (kg)

Calculate the basic energy requirements of the three people listed in the table below.

Name	Body mass (kg)	Basic energy requirement (kJ/day)
Ben	85	
Sam	70	
Elizabeth	65	

b) State **one** factor, apart from body mass, that affects how much energy a person needs each day.

....

Top Tips: Unfortunately there's a bit of maths creeping into this section but don't panic, it's nothing too tricky. If you need to calculate someone's daily energy requirement or their body mass index (see the next page) all you have to do is write down the right formula and stick the numbers in.

Energy Needs

Q3 Stella is an **athlete** — she runs and cycles as part of her endurance training. Stella's **personal trainer** has assessed her basic energy requirement per day (i.e. before any exercise) as **8000 kJ**. Running requires **1500 kJ** per hour, and cycling requires **750 kJ** per hour.

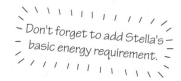

Below is Stella's exercise diary for three days.

> Monday — 2 hour run
>
> Tuesday — cycled for 3 hours
>
> Wednesday — ran for one hour, cycled for 2 hours

Don't forget to add Stella's basic energy requirement.

Work out Stella's **energy requirement** for each day.

a) Monday ....

b) Tuesday ....

c) Wednesday ....

Q4 The **body mass index** (BMI) is an indicator of whether a person is **underweight**, **normal** or **overweight**. It is calculated using the formula below and the table shows how people are categorised according to their BMI.

BMI	weight description
below 18.5	underweight
18.5-24.9	normal
25-29.9	overweight
30-40	moderately obese
over 40	severely obese

$$BMI = body\ mass\ (kg) \div height^2\ (m)$$

a) Calculate the **BMI** for the following people and indicate which weight description each should have.

Name	Height (m)	Mass (kg)	BMI	Weight description
Jenny	1.5	70		
Hannah	1.7	60		
Paul	1.8	55		
Chris	1.8	91		

b) Will is a rugby player and his BMI assessment classes him as 'overweight'. His trainer advises him not to worry about it and to continue with his current diet and exercise regime. Suggest a reason behind the trainer's advice.

....

Muscle weighs more than fat — think about what this will do to the calculation.

....

Finding the Optimum Diet

Q1 Gary works in an **office** and does relatively **little exercise**. His friend Dan plays professional **rugby league**. Their **diets** are very different.

a) Who should eat more **kilojoules (kJ)** per day? Circle the correct answer.

     Dan   Gary   they should eat the same amount

b) Dan eats more **protein** than Gary. Why is eating protein important for athletes? Circle the correct answer.

    To build and repair muscle.   To stay hydrated.   To help regulate body temperature.

c) Dan and Gary's friend Chris is a **marathon runner**.
Draw lines to match each person to the amount of **carbohydrate** they should be eating each day.

Dan	375 g/day
Gary	700 g/day
Chris	1000 g/day

Q2 Flatmates Bernie and Craig go to see a **dietician** called Phil. Phil offers to analyse their diets. Bernie is a keen **body builder** but Craig does much **less exercise**. They give Phil their **24-hour diet recalls** but, because they have spent the day together in their flat, the food they have eaten is virtually the same. Phil's comments, however, are different for each person.

Here is their 24-hour dietary recall.

8.00: two slices of toast, cup of coffee (Bernie had jam on his toast)
10.30: pack of crisps, cup of coffee
13.00: fish and chips, can of cola
15.00: slice of cake, cup of tea
19.00: chicken curry, rice, salad, glass of beer
23.00: cup of coffee

Below are some of Phil's comments. Circle the answers to show whether the comments are likely to apply to Bernie, Craig, or both, considering their different lifestyles.

a) "You are not eating enough protein."   **Bernie / Craig / both**

b) "You need to cut down on the amount of kilojoules you consume."   **Bernie / Craig / both**

c) "You need more fruit and vegetables."   **Bernie / Craig / both**

d) "Your diet is too high in fat."   **Bernie / Craig / both**

Finding the Optimum Diet

Q3 Nicola is hoping to be an Olympic **swimmer**. Her coach has asked a **sports nutritionist** to advise her on her diet. Below is Nicola's **24-hour dietary recall** — a list of everything that she ate in 24 hours. The nutritionist's comments are written alongside.

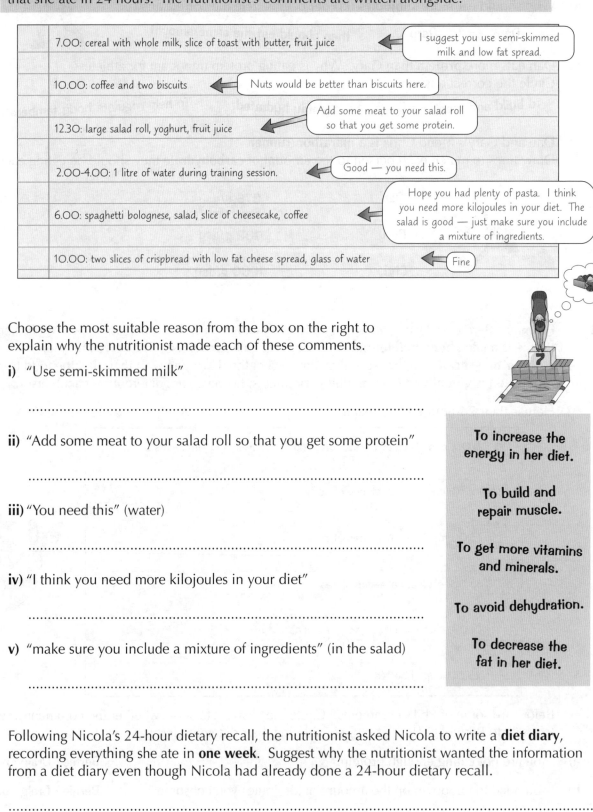

7.00: cereal with whole milk, slice of toast with butter, fruit juice ← I suggest you use semi-skimmed milk and low fat spread.

10.00: coffee and two biscuits ← Nuts would be better than biscuits here.

12.30: large salad roll, yoghurt, fruit juice ← Add some meat to your salad roll so that you get some protein.

2.00-4.00: 1 litre of water during training session. ← Good — you need this.

6.00: spaghetti bolognese, salad, slice of cheesecake, coffee ← Hope you had plenty of pasta. I think you need more kilojoules in your diet. The salad is good — just make sure you include a mixture of ingredients.

10.00: two slices of crispbread with low fat cheese spread, glass of water ← Fine

a) Choose the most suitable reason from the box on the right to explain why the nutritionist made each of these comments.

   i) "Use semi-skimmed milk"

   ....

   ii) "Add some meat to your salad roll so that you get some protein"

   ....

   iii) "You need this" (water)

   ....

   iv) "I think you need more kilojoules in your diet"

   ....

   v) "make sure you include a mixture of ingredients" (in the salad)

   ....

> To increase the energy in her diet.
>
> To build and repair muscle.
>
> To get more vitamins and minerals.
>
> To avoid dehydration.
>
> To decrease the fat in her diet.

b) Following Nicola's 24-hour dietary recall, the nutritionist asked Nicola to write a **diet diary**, recording everything she ate in **one week**. Suggest why the nutritionist wanted the information from a diet diary even though Nicola had already done a 24-hour dietary recall.

....

....

Section 2 — Health, Exercise and Nutrition

Energy Rich and Muscle Building Diets

Q1 Phil is a keen **bodybuilder**. Each day he takes a high **protein** drink in addition to his normal diet.

a) Why would a bodybuilder benefit from taking extra **protein**? Circle the correct answer.

To increase the strength of their bones.   To increase muscle mass.

b) Which of the following **foods** would you recommend to Phil to boost his protein intake? Circle the correct answer.

meat   fruit   rice

Q2 Some **sports scientists** were investigating the effect of an athlete's **pre-event diet** on **performance** in **long distance running** events. They used three groups of 20 athletes.

> **Group 1** ate a diet low in complex carbohydrates for one week.
>
> **Group 2** ate the same amount of kilojoules as group 1 but had a balanced diet with a normal level of complex carbohydrates for one week.
>
> **Group 3** ate the same amount of kilojoules as groups 1 and 2 but had a high percentage of complex carbohydrates for one week.

Each member of each group then ran on a treadmill, set at a fixed speed, until they were exhausted. The time taken to reach exhaustion was measured. The average results are shown below.

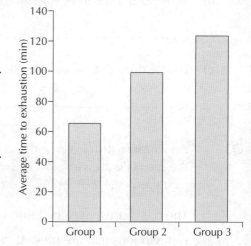

a) From these results, what pre-event diet would you recommend for long distance runners?

....

b) Name **one** step the sports scientists took to ensure this was a fair test.

....

c) Which of the following foods is **not** high in complex carbohydrates? Circle **one** answer.

eggs   bread   pasta

d) Complete the passage below using the words in the box.

glycogen	'carbohydrate loading'	energy	muscle stiffness	broken down

Carbohydrates are .... in the body to release glucose. Excess glucose can be stored in the muscles as a chemical called .... When the muscles need more energy, this is converted back into glucose, which is broken down to release .... The amount of glycogen stored in their muscles can be increased by ...., so athletes can run for longer without getting tired. This can have some side effects though, like .... and chest pains.

Sports Drinks

Q1 Alex is a **footballer**. His trainer advises him to drink an **isotonic sports drink** during strenuous **exercise**.

a) Glucose is one ingredient in isotonic sports drinks.
What are the other **two** main **ingredients**? Circle the correct answers.

protein   water   vitamin C   electrolytes

b) As well as isotonic sports drinks, you can also get **hypertonic** and **hypotonic** sports drinks.
They all contain different amounts of **glucose**. Which of the three types of drinks contains:

i) the **most** glucose ....   **ii)** the **least** glucose ....

iii) Alex is in his last training session of the day but he feels like he doesn't have enough **energy**.
What drink should his coach recommend? Circle the correct answer.

a hypotonic drink   a hypertonic drink

Q2 Louise trains at the gym **once a week**. Sarah trains **three or four times each week**. Sarah drinks an **energy drink** (a water and high sugar drink), whereas Louise just drinks **water**. Their trainer advises Sarah that she should use an **isotonic drink** instead, but says nothing to Louise.

a) Why do both girls need to drink water after they exercise?

....

b) Why does the trainer suggest that Sarah uses an isotonic drink rather than an energy drink?

....

c) Louise doesn't train as often as Sarah. Suggest why Louise doesn't need an isotonic drink.

....

Q3 An **isotonic drink** is advertised as replacing the **ions** (electrolytes) lost in **sweat**.
Its ingredients are displayed on the right.

| sucrose, glucose, maltodextrin, fructose, citric acid, electrolytes (tri sodium citrate, sodium chloride, potassium chloride), flavouring. |

The pie chart shows the ionic composition of sweat.

a) List two ions that are present in **sweat** but are not listed in the ingredients of the drink.

1. ....

2. ....

b) What percentage of the ions in sweat are **potassium**?

....

calcium 1%   magnesium 2%
chloride 50%
sodium 39%
potassium

c) The list of ingredients shows high sucrose and glucose contents.
Suggest **one** possible **negative** effect on health of regularly using a drink that is high in sugar.

....

Mixed Questions for Section 2

Q1   Lyndsey is a **dietician**. The table below shows sample daily plans from three of her **diet plans** for people with **different nutritional needs**.

	PLAN 1	PLAN 2	PLAN 3
Breakfast	cereal with milk, banana, orange juice	four eggs and bacon, fruit juice	cereal with milk, grapefruit juice
Mid-morning	coffee, two slices of wholemeal bread	glass of milk	nothing
Lunch	pasta with sauce, green beans, apple, yoghurt, two wholemeal biscuits	steak and baked potato, glass of water	ham and salad sandwich, apple, fruit juice
Mid-afternoon	banana, cup of tea	nothing	biscuit and cup of tea
Early evening	curry and rice, salad, orange	fish, boiled potatoes, beans, glass of milk	grilled chicken, baked potato, peas, yoghurt
Late evening	two crackers and cheese	protein shake	nothing

a) State which diet plan would be most suitable for each of the following people.

   i)   A weightlifter. ....

   ii) A non-athlete. ....

   iii) An endurance runner. ....

b) Which of the three plans do you think has the highest energy intake? ....

c) What will to happen to an endurance runner if they continue to use this diet plan after a marathon, but cut down the amount of exercise they do? Circle the correct answer.

   They will put on weight.   **They will lose weight.**   **They will stay the same weight.**

Q2   Before starting a **training programme** Jamil weighs **75 kg** and his BMI is **26.3**. He is **1.69 m** tall.

a) Jamil has built up to **rowing** for **two hours** each day. This uses **3265 kJ**. Calculate Jamil's energy requirement for one day.

    Start by working out Jamil's basic energy requirement (BER).

....

....

b) After six months of training Jamil weighs **85 kg**. Calculate Jamil's new BMI.

    The formula for finding BMI is on page 20.

....

....

c) Jamil's trainer thinks that he might have put on weight due to drinking too many **isotonic drinks**. Which ingredient in isotonic drinks contains energy?

....

Mixed Questions for Section 2

Q3　Matt's trainer is assessing his fitness. The trainer gets him to ride on an **exercise bike**. During his ride the trainer measures his **pulse rate**.

The results of Matt's tests are shown in the graph below.

a)　Why did Matt's **pulse rate** go up when he exercised? Complete the following sentence:

> To provide his muscles with more oxygen and glucose needed for ....

b)　**i)** What was Matt's **resting heart rate**?

....

ii) When do you think Matt **stopped exercising**?

....

iii) Give a reason for you answer to part **ii)**.

....

....

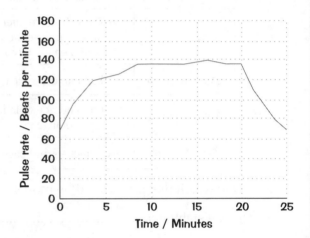

iv) Use the graph to find Matt's **pulse recovery time**. ....

Q4　Rob has **asthma** and often feels out of breath. He is taking part in a **scientific study** to see if regular **swimming** can help improve his asthma.

a)　Fill in the blanks to complete this passage on the respiratory system.

intercostal muscles	trachea	alveoli

> The .... is a tube which connects your nose and
> mouth to your lungs. The .... move your ribs
> up and down during breathing. The .... are
> air sacs in the lungs where carbon dioxide is exchanged for oxygen.

b)　As part of the study a **sports physiologist** will take regular measurements of Rob's **lung capacity**. Circle the correct words from each pair to complete the following paragraph.

> To measure your **tidal volume / vital capacity** you should breathe normally
> into the spirometer three times and then divide the reading by three to find
> your average. To measure your **tidal volume / vital capacity** you should
> breathe in as far as you can, and then breathe out as far as you can.
> Repeat the exercise two more times and use the **highest / lowest** value.

Mixed Questions for Section 2

Q5 **Sports scientists** wanted to study what happens to the human body during a **marathon race**. They decided to measure **various factors** in a runner's body at different points during the race.

a) In the table below tick one box in each row to indicate what you would expect to happen to each of the factors that the scientists measure during the race.

Factor to be measured	Goes up	Goes down
Breathing rate		
Heart rate		
Blood glucose level		
Stores of glycogen in the liver		
Amount of sweating		

b) Marathon runners rarely need to stop to **urinate** during a race even though it takes several hours to complete. Suggest a reason for this.

....

c) i) Name **one** way the scientists could measure blood glucose levels.

....

ii) Name **one** hormone that helps to control glucose levels. ....

d) The blood vessels that supply the skin capillaries can change width to regulate body temperature. What do you think would happen to these blood vessels during a marathon?

....

Q6 Viki injured herself playing tennis. Her **physiotherapist** diagnosed the injury as a tear in her **biceps**.

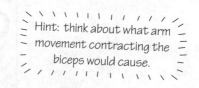

Hint: think about what arm movement contracting the biceps would cause.

a) From looking at the way the muscle is connected, which **symptom** is Viki most likely to suffer from when her biceps is injured? Tick the **one** correct answer.

☐ Pain when unclenching her fist.

☐ Pain when hunching her shoulders.

☐ Pain when moving her forearm.

☐ Pain when clenching her fist.

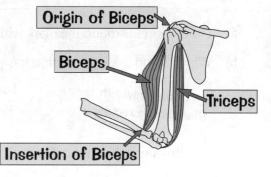

b) The triceps is the antagonist muscle to the biceps. Explain what is meant by **antagonistic muscles**. ....

....

Product Standards

Q1 New products and materials are tested to make sure they are **high quality** and **fit for purpose**.

a) Draw lines to match the terms 'high quality' and 'fit for purpose' with their definitions.

High quality   Will do the job it claims to do

Fit for purpose   Safe and reliable

b) The **BSI** is an organisation responsible for setting and testing product standards.

   i) What does BSI stand for?

   ....

   ii) If a product has been tested by the BSI, which of these logos will be displayed on the product? Circle the correct answer.

Q2 The diagram below shows a sticker that Henry found on the back of his **stereo**.

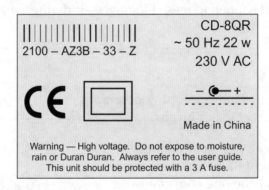

a) Draw a circle around the mark which shows that the stereo conforms to a set of safety standards.

b) Which standards organisation has certified this stereo as safe? Circle the correct answer.

   Commonwealth Standards Executives

   European Committee for Standardisation

   International Organisation for Standards

c) Can this stereo be sold in Europe? Explain your answer.

   ....

   ....

Mechanical Properties

Q1 Circle the correct word in each pair to show whether the following diagrams show objects under **compression** or **tension**.

a)

The cable is under

tension / compression.

b)

The nail is under

tension / compression.

c)

The hinges of a very full suitcase are under

tension / compression.

The clothes inside it are under

tension / compression.

Q2 Draw lines to connect each **mechanical property** with the correct **definition**.

Flexibility

Density

Hardness

a material's resistance to scratching and indentation

how easily a material's shape can be changed

how much mass there is in a given volume

Q3 The statements below are about the **mechanical properties** of materials.

Tick the boxes to show whether the statements are **true** or **false**.

	True	False
a) Stiff materials don't change shape much under a large load.	☐	☐
b) A brittle material can deform quite a lot without breaking.	☐	☐
c) A material can be tough as well as brittle.	☐	☐
d) A material can be tough as well as flexible.	☐	☐
e) Dense materials are used to make lightweight sports equipment.	☐	☐

Q4 Pablo needs to choose a material to make a **fishing rod**.

What **mechanical properties** should the material he chooses have? Tick the boxes next to the **three** correct answers.

Low density ☐ Flexibility ☐ Brittleness ☐

Stiffness ☐ Toughness ☐ High density ☐

Section 3 — Materials and Their Properties

Mechanical Properties

Q5 Kelly works for a company that designs **pole vault poles**.
The materials used to make the poles have to have certain **properties**.

a) Kelly says that the **density** of the material needs to be as low as possible. Explain why.

....

b) The pole needs to bend and straighten many times without breaking.
What **mechanical property** does the material need to be able to do this?

....

c) The diagram below shows a pole vault pole in use. Complete the diagram by labelling
which part of the pole is under **compression** and which part is under **tension**.

B

A

Think about what is happening to the material at point A and point B. Is it being stretched or squashed?

Q6 Materials can be **strong** in different ways.

a) Draw lines to connect each type of strength with its correct definition.

Tensile strength

Compressive strength

The ability to resist stretching.

The ability to resist crushing or squashing.

b) **Concrete** is used to make the foundations of houses. What type of strength does concrete
need to have to make it suitable for this use? Explain your answer.

....

....

c) **Steel** is used to make the towbars that connect cars to caravans. What type of strength
does steel need to have to make it suitable for this use? Explain your answer.

....

....

Measuring Mechanical Properties

Q1   Hugo is investigating the **stiffness** of three different materials.

a) The diagram below shows the apparatus that Hugo uses to compare the stiffness of the different materials. Label the diagram using the words in the box.

| Ruler | Material under test | Load | Pulley | Paper marker |

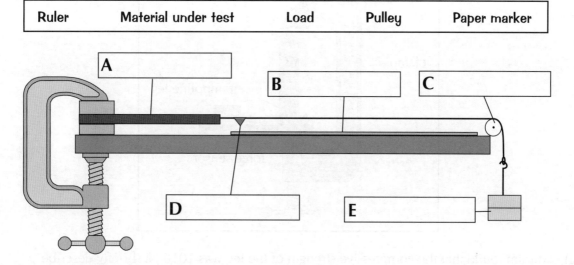

Hugo adds a range of different **loads** to samples of each of the three materials. He measures how much each material stretches (the **extension**) with each load.

b) Hugo makes sure that all the samples he uses are the **same length** and **thickness**. Why does he do this? Circle the correct answer.

So the materials look the same   So it is a fair test   To make his results more precise   So he can't tell the materials apart

c) Hugo decides to compare the different materials by plotting a **force-extension graph**. A graph of Hugo's results is shown here.

i) Which material has the **lowest** stiffness?

....

ii) When a force of **350 N** was applied to material C, its length increased by **0.2 cm**. Calculate the **stiffness constant** for material C.

Force = Constant × Extension

....

....

The first thing you need to do is rearrange the equation.

d) Describe how Hugo could use the same apparatus to measure the **tensile strength** of a sample.

....

....

Measuring Mechanical Properties

Q2 Miriam works for a company that makes **trampolines**. She is testing the **compressive strength** of the leg of an indoor trampoline, using the apparatus shown below.

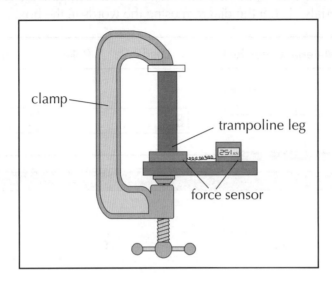

clamp

trampoline leg

force sensor

a) Miriam found that the compressive strength of the leg was 1010 N. Briefly describe how Miriam will have used the apparatus shown above to get this result.

....

....

....

b) The cross-sectional area of the trampoline leg is 50 cm². Calculate the stress that would have to be applied to the trampoline leg for it to break.

$$\text{Stress} = \frac{\text{Force}}{\text{Cross-sectional Area}}$$

....

....

c) The trampoline legs produced by a rival trampoline company break when a stress of **20 N/cm²** is applied. Is the material that these legs are made from **stronger** or **weaker** than the material that Miriam's trampoline legs are made from? Explain your answer.

....

....

Top Tips: It's dead important that you don't get compressive and tensile strengths muddled up. They're two different things and they're measured in two completely different ways. Make sure that you can describe the methods (and recognise all the apparatus) used for measuring both of them.

Measuring Mechanical Properties

Q3 A materials scientist has developed a new material. He wants to test the **hardness** and **toughness** of the material compared to stainless steel.

Yep, physics is pretty hard.

a) To test **hardness**, the scientist drops a weight down a tube on to a nail that's resting on a sample of the material. When the weight hits the nail, it dents the material. How is the **hardness** of the material related to the **size of the dent**?

....

b) The **toughness** of both materials can be measured using an **impact test**. Complete the passage on impact tests by circling the correct word in each pair.

> Put a **groove / nail** into the material. Break the material by swinging a pendulum hammer from a **set / random** height. Measure how high the pendulum hammer swings **before / after** the material is broken. Tough materials absorb **less / more** energy when they break than brittle materials. This means the pendulum hammer will have **less / more** energy after breaking the material. So the tougher the material the **higher / lower** the pendulum hammer will swing.

c) When the material is left in **water** for a long period of time it becomes **brittle**. What does this tell you about the material? Tick the box next to the correct answer.

The material is resistant to corrosion. ☐   The material has a low density. ☐

The material is not resistant to corrosion. ☐   The material has a high density. ☐

Q4 A piece of material has a volume of **0.0004 m³** and a mass of **550 g**.

a) Describe how the volume and the mass of the piece of material could have been measured.

Volume: ....

....

Mass: ....

b) Calculate the **density** of the material in **kg/m³**.

$$\text{Density} = \frac{\text{Mass}}{\text{Volume}}$$

Density is measured in kg/m³, so the mass has to be in kg and the volume has to be in m³.

....

....

Measuring Electrical and Thermal Properties

Q1 Michael is developing a new product and needs a material that has a **high electrical conductivity**.

You can compare the electrical conductivities of different materials by putting a piece of each material into a circuit and measuring the **current** flowing through it.

a) What device can be used to measure the current flowing through a circuit?
Circle the correct answer.

Voltmeter   Thermometer   Force Sensor   Diode   Ammeter

b) The table below shows the results for three materials that Michael tested.

Material	Current (A)
A	0.65
B	2.40
C	0.01

Look at the size of the current. That'll tell you how good an electrical conductor the material is.

i) Which material has the **highest** electrical conductivity?

....

ii) Which material could be described as an electrical **insulator**?

....

Q2 Pans are usually made out of metal because metals have a **high thermal conductivity**.

a) What is **thermal conductivity**?

....

b) The passage below describes how the thermal conductivity of a material can be measured.
Complete the passage using the words in the box. You won't have to use all the words.

thermometer	clamp	high	ammeter	flame	low

Put one end of the material into a .... Measure the

temperature of the other end of the material using a ....

Time how long it takes for the material to reach a particular temperature.

Materials with a .... thermal conductivity will take less

time for the temperature of the other end to heat up.

c) A scientist wants to compare the thermal conductivity of two materials.
Suggest **one** thing the scientist could do to make sure it's a **fair test**.

....

Ceramics

Q1 Ceramic materials have a number of common features.

Tick the boxes to show whether the following statements about the properties of ceramics are **true** or **false**.

	True	False
a) Ceramics are very soft.	☐	☐
b) Ceramics are brittle — they break when bent.	☐	☐
c) Ceramics won't react with many chemicals.	☐	☐
d) Ceramics are poor conductors of heat.	☐	☐
e) Ceramics will melt at relatively low temperatures.	☐	☐

Q2 The **heat-resistant tiles** on space shuttles are made using **ceramic materials**.

a) Why do space shuttles need heat-resistant tiles?
Tick the box next to the correct answer.

To keep the astronauts warm in space where it is very cold. ☐

To protect the astronauts from high temperatures when they are near the Sun. ☐

To protect the astronauts from high temperatures when the shuttle re-enters the Earth's atmosphere. ☐

b) i) Suggest **two** properties of ceramic materials that make them good materials to use for making heat-resistant tiles.

1. ....

2. ....

ii) Explain why these are good properties for heat-resistant tiles to have.

....

....

Q3 Ceramic materials are sometimes used to make **artificial joints**.

Three properties of ceramic materials are listed below. Explain why each property makes ceramics good materials to use for making artificial joints.

Durable: ....

Smooth: ....

Resistant to chemical attack: ....

Metals

Q1 The atoms in metals are held together by **metallic bonds**.

a) The diagram below shows the arrangement of the particles in a typical **metal**.
Label the diagram using the words in the box below.

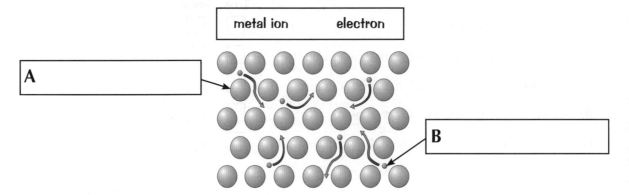

| metal ion | electron |

A

B

b) Circle the phrase which best describes **metallic bonding**.

Strong attractions between negative
electrons and positive metal ions.

Weak attractions between positive
electrons and negative metal ions.

Strong attractions between positive
electrons and negative metal ions.

Weak attractions between negative
electrons and positive metal ions.

Q2 John is a materials scientist working for a company that **designs sports equipment**.
He often uses **metals** or **alloys** as materials in his designs, because of their useful properties.

a) Draw lines to match the properties of metals and alloys to their correct meanings.

High tensile strength

Flexible

Hard

Good conductors of heat

Heat energy can flow through them easily.

They are hard to break when being stretched.

They are difficult to dent when pressure is applied.

They can bend easily without breaking.

b) The following pieces of sports equipment are made of metal.
Circle the **main reason** why metal is used for each type of equipment.

i) The pointed end of a dart   It has a low tensile strength. / It is hard.

ii) Springs in a trampoline   They are flexible. / They are strong.

iii) Support wires holding up a tennis net   They have a high tensile strength. / They are flexible.

Top Tips: If you're asked whether a metal would be a good material to make a certain object
from, think about the properties it would need and see if they match up with the properties of the metal.

Section 3 — Materials and Their Properties

Metals

Q3 Tick the boxes to show whether the following statements about **alloys** are **true** or **false**.

True False

a) An alloy is a mixture of two or more elements. ☐ ☐

b) Both of the elements in an alloy must be metals. ☐ ☐

c) The atoms in an alloy are arranged in regular layers. ☐ ☐

d) Alloys are usually harder than pure metals. ☐ ☐

e) Aluminium alloys are used to make aircraft frames. ☐ ☐

Alloy there matey!

Q4 The passage below explains why **titanium** is a good material to use for making high-performance bicycle frames.

Complete the passage using the words in the box.

low density	strong	lightweight	corrosion resistant	rusty

Titanium is .... so the bicycle frame won't break easily.

Titanium is .... so the bicycle frame will not go

.... if it is used outdoors.

Titanium has a .... so the bicycle frame will

be .... and go faster.

Q5 The properties of metals are due to their **bonding**.

Use your knowledge of **metallic bonding** and how the atoms in a metal are **arranged** to explain why metals have the following properties.

a) High tensile strength:

....

....

b) High thermal conductivity:

....

....

c) Malleability:

Malleable means it can be hammered into shape and rolled into sheets.

....

....

Polymers

Q1 Polymers have plenty of useful properties. Circle the correct word in each pair to complete the sentences about the properties of polymers.

Some proper ties

a) Polymers have a **low** / **high** density. This is because the chains in polymers are **branched** / **straight** so they **can** / **can't** pack together very tightly.

b) Polymers are usually quite **flexible** / **rigid**. This is because the bonds between the chains are **strong** / **weak** so the chains **can** / **can't** easily slide across one another as the polymer bends.

c) Polymers have a **low** / **high** thermal conductivity. This is because the chains in polymers are **loosely** / **tightly** packed so heat energy is transferred **quickly** / **slowly**.

Q2 The passage below describes the structure of a **polymer**.

Complete the passage using the words in the box.

One of these words is used twice.

atoms	weak	strong	chains

Polymers are made up of .... , which are joined together

to form long ....

Lots of .... pack together side by side.

The atoms are held together by .... covalent bonds.

The chains are held together by .... forces of attraction.

Q3 Berengere designs sporty new **bicycle helmets**. Her latest design uses two different **polymers** — one for the outer casing and another for the inner lining. Decide whether the following properties are needed for the **inner lining**, **outer casing** or **both**. Draw a ring around the correct option.

a) Lightweight   inner lining / outer casing / both

b) Hard   inner lining / outer casing / both   outer casing

c) Water-resistant   inner lining / outer casing / both   inner lining

d) Flexible   inner lining / outer casing / both

Q4 Kevlar® is a type of polymer. It is **light**, **strong** and can **absorb lots of energy** without breaking.

Suggest two pieces of sports equipment that Kevlar® could be used to make.

1. ....

2. ....

Polymers

Q5 **Thermoplastic polymers** and **thermosetting polymers** have different properties.

a) Draw lines to join each type of polymer to the description of the bonding between its chains.

Thermoplastic polymer

Thermosetting polymer

Very weak forces of attraction between the chains.

Strong cross-links between the chains.

b) i) Which type of polymer can easily be melted and remoulded? Circle the correct answer.

Thermoplastic polymer   Thermosetting polymer

ii) Which type of polymer remains rigid once set? Circle the correct answer.

Thermoplastic polymer   Thermosetting polymer

Rigid is the opposite of flexible.

Q6 The forces of attraction between the chains of a polymer are affected by the **structure** of the polymer.

Tick the boxes to show whether the following statements are **true** or **false**.

	True	False
a) Long chains are held together more strongly than shorter chains.	☐	☐
b) Branched chains are held together more strongly than unbranched chains.	☐	☐
c) Polymers with weaker forces between the chains are stronger.	☐	☐
d) Polymers with stronger forces between the chains are denser.	☐	☐
e) Polymers with stronger forces between the chains have lower melting points.	☐	☐

Q7 Kirsty works in the **materials** department of a **sports equipment manufacturer**. She needs to choose materials for three different projects. Below is a list of her requirements for each project.

Project A — Material needs to be strong, flexible and high density.
Project B — Material needs to be flexible, low density and insulate heat well.
Project C — Material needs to have a low density and a high thermal conductivity.

a) Kirsty recommended a **polymer** for one of the projects. Which project could this be? ....

b) For each of the other two projects, give one reason why Kirsty did **not** recommend a polymer.

Project: .... Reason: ....

Project: .... Reason: ....

Composites

Q1 Circle the statement below that best describes a **composite material**.

a material made of lots of molecules
joined together in long chains

a very light and flexible material

a very expensive material

a material made of two or more different materials

Q2 Darren is choosing a new bicycle wheel for his **racing bike**. He looks at a **steel wheel** and a wheel made from **carbon reinforced plastic** (CRP). CRP has a **low density** and is **very strong**.

steel wheel   CRP wheel

This page is a bit of an uphill struggle.

a) What is the main **advantage** of using the CRP wheel?

....

b) Suggest why the CRP wheel only needs three spokes.

....

c) CRP is made from **plastic** and **carbon fibres**. For each one of the properties below, decide whether they are due to the plastic or the carbon. Circle the correct answer.

i) low density   **plastic / carbon**

ii) very strong   **plastic / carbon**

Q3 Lewis is a racing car driver. His brakes are made from **ceramics** and **carbon**.

a) Decide whether the properties of the brakes below are due to the **ceramics** or the **carbon**. Circle the correct answer.

i) They are durable so they don't wear down too quickly.   **ceramics / carbon**

ii) They have a high melting point so they don't melt when they get hot.   **ceramics / carbon**

iii) They are lightweight, which helps the car go faster.   **ceramics / carbon**

b) i) Lewis's car has a laminated windscreen. What is the structure of a laminated windscreen? Tick the box next to the correct answer.

Two layers of glass with a layer of plastic in between. ☐

Two layers of plastic with a layer of glass in between. ☐

One layer of glass and one layer of plastic. ☐

laminated windscreen

ceramic-carbon brakes

ii) Why are laminated windscreens safer than windscreens made with just glass?

....

Choosing the Best Material

Q1 Materials can be **natural** or **synthetic**.

a) Draw lines to match the types of materials to their definitions.

Natural material   A material that is found in the environment.

Synthetic material   A material which is man-made.

b) Put the materials listed below into the table to show whether they are natural or synthetic. Two have been done for you.

wood   polyethene   wool   silk   carbon reinforced plastic   polystyrene

Natural Materials	Synthetic Materials
metal	fiberglass

c) Which of the following are advantages of using **synthetic materials** over natural materials? Circle the correct answers.

They are often cheaper

They can be more durable

They are easy to dispose of

They come from sustainable sources

You can make them in whatever shape you need

Their properties can be changed to meet your needs

Q2 Different properties of materials are **desirable** for different purposes.

Desirable properties are properties that are useful.

Draw lines to match up the properties with why they are desirable.

smooth   lightweight

low density   keeps things hot or cold

low thermal conductivity   can withstand big forces

shock-absorbing   can bend and stretch

flexible   reduces friction

Top Tips: There's usually more than one reason why a particular material is chosen to make a particular product. Manufacturers have to think about the cost and availability of materials, as well as their properties when deciding which materials to use. So choosing the best material can be a tad tricky.

Choosing the Best Material

Q3   **Style For Sport** is a company that makes **sportswear** and **sports equipment**. They take special care to choose the right **materials** for the purpose of each product.

Below is a list of some of the materials they use to make their sportswear, and the properties of those materials. Write down the material most suitable for **clothing** used in the sports below.

Material	Properties
Cotton	Comfortable, light, soft
Leather	Tough, durable, strong
Elastane	Stretchy, durable
Polyester-cotton mix	Waterproof, breathable

a)   Tennis ....

c)   Gymnastics ....

b)   Sailing ....

d)   Motorcycling ....

Q4   Jake is a **sports car designer**. He is researching the **properties** of some **metals** that he is thinking about using for his cars. Below is his table showing the properties of each metal.

Metal	Density (g/cm³)	Tensile strength (MPa)	Melting point (°C)
Aluminium	2.7	90	660
Cobalt	8.9	225	1495
Steel	7.9	285	825
Titanium	4.5	220	1668

That's my house.

a)   Which metal is the **strongest**? ....

b)   The high performance engines in sports cars get very **hot**.
Why is **titanium** a good material for Jake to use in his high performance engine?

....

c)   It's important that the engine in a sports car is not too **heavy**.
Why is **cobalt** a bad material for Jake to use in a sports car engine?

....

d)   Jake also designs **go-karts**. Go-karts need to be **lightweight** so they can go really fast. Which metal from the table should be used to make the **fastest** go-karts? Give a reason for your answer.

Metal: ....

Reason: ....

Mixed Questions for Section 3

Q1 Stephanie is making a list of the main **properties** of various materials. Choose from the properties below to complete the table. You can use properties more than once.

high melting point   high tensile strength   low density   flexible

low thermal conductivity   high thermal conductivity

Material	Characteristic properties
Metals	
Ceramics	
Polymers	

Q2 **Tennis racquets** used to be made of **wood**, but today are made from **composite** materials. Here is a picture of a modern tennis racquet and one that people used about 30 years ago.

modern tennis racquet

old-fashioned tennis racquet

a) Give **one** reason why the material that a product is made of might change over time.

....

....

b) Modern racquet frames use **composite** materials. Circle the correct word from the pair to explain how this has enabled manufacturers to build racquets with bigger heads.

Composite materials are **stronger / weaker** than wood, meaning
that they can keep the strings in tension over a larger area.

c) **Steel** is very strong. What would be the main **disadvantage** of building tennis racquets from steel?

....

Mixed Questions for Section 3

Q3 Stephen is a materials scientist. He has developed a new material which he thinks could be used to make crash helmets for motorbikes.

I should invent a better crash helmet.

a) Crash helmets need to have **high compressive strength**.

   i) What is compressive strength?

   ....

   ii) Number the sentences below (1-5) to show how Stephen could test the compressive strength of his new material. The first one has been done for you.

   ☐ Start to gradually tighten the clamp.

   ☐ Keep tightening the clamp until the material breaks.

   1 Put the material in a clamp with a force sensor.

   ☐ Take a reading from the force sensor.

   ☐ The reading on the force sensor is the compressive strength.

b) Some other properties of Stephen's new material are listed below. Which **two** of these properties make Stephen's new material good for making crash helmets? Explain your answers.

   high tensile strength   shock-absorbing   high melting point   low density   low thermal conductivity

   1. Property: ....

   Explanation: ....

   2. Property: ....

   Explanation: ....

c) The material that Stephen has developed is synthetic.
   Give **one disadvantage** of using a synthetic material over a natural material.

   ....

   ....

d) A crash helmet made from Stephen's new material would need to meet the standards set by the **European Committee for Standardisation** before it could be sold in Europe.

   i) Which logo will be displayed on the helmet after it has met these standards?
   Circle the correct answer.

   ♡®   CE   ECS   ♻®   Ϛ

   ii) Name another standards organisation that could test the new helmet before it is sold in the UK.

   ....

Mixed Questions for Section 3

Q4 Sunni is investigating the properties of two **alloys** — alloy A and alloy B.

a) What is an alloy? Circle the correct answer.

A mixture of two or more elements where at least one of the elements is a metal.

A mixture of two or more elements where neither of the elements are metals.

A mixture of two or more elements where both of the elements are metals.

b) Sunni put a piece of each of the alloys in turn into a **circuit** with an **ammeter**. The reading on the ammeter was **much higher** for alloy B than for alloy A. What does this tell you about alloy B?

A high ammeter reading means there's lots of current flowing through the circuit.

....

c) Describe a test that Sunni could do to compare the **thermal conductivity** of the two alloys.

....

....

....

d) Sunni did an impact test on both alloys, and found that alloy A was **tougher** than alloy B. If a material is described as **tough** what does this mean? Tick the box next to the correct answer.

The material breaks before it deforms. ☐   The material is resistant to scratching. ☐

The material can deform without breaking. ☐   The material is not resistant to scratching. ☐

e) A piece of alloy B with a volume of **30 cm³** has a mass of **210 g**. Calculate the density of alloy B in **g/cm³**.

$$\text{Density} = \frac{\text{Mass}}{\text{Volume}}$$

....

....

Q5 **Cermet** is a mixture of a ceramic material and a metal. It is both **malleable** and **heat resistant**. It's used to make a heat-resistant coating for the engines in some sports cars.

a) Is cermet a composite or a polymer? ....

b) Which part of the mixture makes the cermet malleable? Circle the correct answer.

The ceramic   The metal

c) Explain why a metal or a ceramic by itself wouldn't be suitable for this purpose.

....

....

....

Agricultural and Food Scientists

Q1 Agricultural scientists are interested in some areas of **biotechnology**.
What do they use biotechnology for? Circle the **two** correct answers.

To alter the genes of
sheep to try and turn them
different colours.

To alter the genes of plants and
crops to make them grow with
a higher yield.

To alter the genes of plants
and crops to make them more
resistant to disease.

To alter the genes of
cows to make them
produce flavoured milk.

Q2 **Agricultural** and **food scientists** do a wide range of jobs.

a) Tick the **four** correct boxes to show the things that agricultural scientists do.

Look after water supplies. ☐

Study humans to try and cure diseases. ☐

Study how to maintain good quality soil. ☐

Study how to get rid of pests and weeds. ☐

Investigate samples taken from crime scenes. ☐

Study animals and crops to improve their quality and yield. ☐

b) Give **one** example of a food scientist working in the **sport industry**.

....

Q3 Food production is **regulated**.

a) There are three important **reasons** why food production is regulated.
Tick the **three** correct boxes below to show what these reasons are.

For public health and safety. ☐

To protect the rights of shop keepers. ☐

For animal welfare. ☐

To protect homeowners. ☐

To protect supermarket interests. ☐

To protect the environment. ☐

b) Name **one** organisation that helps to regulate food production.

....

Food Poisoning

Q1 Eesha has food poisoning. Circle the three **symptoms** that she is likely to have.

stomach pains   swollen feet   blurred vision   toothache

diarrhoea   vomiting   sore throat

Q2 Martin runs **basic food hygiene** courses for people who handle food. Tick the boxes to show whether each of the statements about **food poisoning** is true or false.

		True	False
a)	Food poisoning is caused by microorganisms in food.	☐	☐
b)	Some bacteria make you feel ill because they produce toxins.	☐	☐
c)	*E.coli* bacteria can cause food poisoning.	☐	☐
d)	*Salmonella* can cause food poisoning.	☐	☐
e)	*Campylobacter* can't cause food poisoning.	☐	☐
f)	If you get food poisoning, how ill you get depends on the type of microorganisms you are infected with.	☐	☐
g)	Food poisoning always lasts for exactly one day.	☐	☐

Q3 Susan works as a **quality control manager** for 'Lazy Lettuce', a company that produces pre-packed salads. She assesses the factory for **hygiene problems**.

a) List **two** things that could **contaminate** the salads in the factory.

1. ....   2. ....

b) It is very important that Lazy Lettuce's products **aren't contaminated**.
Complete the passage below using the words from the box.

recall	injured	allergies	label	damaging

If food is contaminated people can get ill or .... The manufacturer

will have to .... the product, which can be expensive and

.... to the company's reputation. Manufacturers must also tell you

on the .... exactly what's in (or could be in) the food, especially if

any ingredients (e.g. peanuts or wheat) could trigger ....

Top Tips: Not a very pleasant topic this one, but it's all stuff you've got to know. Sorry guys. Make sure you learn the causes and symptoms of food poisoning, and just hope that you never get it...

Food Hygiene

Q1   Ami has just started working in a **sandwich shop**. She doesn't know anything about food hygiene.

a)   On the picture of Ami below, circle **four** things that are **unhygienic**.

Hint: Look at what Ami is wearing.

b)   Write down **one** occasion when Ami should **wash her hands** whilst at work.

    ....

c)   At the end of each day, Ami helps to clean the food containers, food preparation surfaces and floors. She uses both **detergents** and **disinfectants**.

    i)   Draw lines to match the chemicals with the job they do.

             Detergent   **A chemical that kills microorganisms.**

             Disinfectant   **A chemical that cleans away grease, oil and dirt.**

    ii) Which of the following cleaning methods could Ami use to make sure any microorganisms in the food containers are **completely destroyed**? Circle **two** correct answers.

       Heat sterilisation   **Wiping the inside of the**   **Sterilisation**
         using steam   **containers with soapy water**   **using radiation**

d)   Ami regularly empties the rubbish bins. Give **one** reason why this keeps the kitchen hygienic.

    ....

e)   Food shops, like the one Ami works in, are in danger of becoming infected by **pests**.
    In the table below, tick the box for the best method of removal for each pest.

	Glueboard	UV light trap	Poison
Mice			
Cockroaches			
Flies			

Food Preservation

Q1 **Restaurants** need to make sure they store food at the correct temperature so that it is safe to eat.

a) Circle the correct word in each pair to complete the sentences below.

> Bacteria that cause food poisoning prefer **dry** / **moist** conditions to grow in.
>
> They also need a good source of **food** / **light**.
>
> For optimal growth, they need a **warm** / **cold** environment.

b) Complete the passage on **food storage** using the words in the box below.

spores	kills	cooling	bacteria	cold	heating	moisture

To store food safely you need to create conditions that will slow down or stop the growth

of .... Fridges are .... to slow down their

growth. Freezing food freezes the .... which they need to grow

and multiply. Cooking food .... them because it gets too hot.

In industry, ultra-heat treatment (UHT) is used. This involves ....

foods for one minute and then .... them really quickly. This

destroys any microorganisms and their ....

Q2 Mark is planning a **camping trip** and needs to take food that **won't go off** if left in his rucksack for several days. His friend suggests taking **dried foods** like rice, packet soups, dried fruits and dried meat.

For this question think about the conditions that bacteria like.

a) Dried foods have had all the **moisture removed** from them.
Explain why this means that Mark is safe to store dried foods in his rucksack.

....

b) Mark decides to take **tinned vegetables** and **pickled onions** instead.

i) Tinned vegetables often contain **brine** (salt water).
How does the salt help stop the vegetables going off?

....

....

ii) Vinegar is **acidic**. Why does pickling onions in **vinegar** stop them from going off?

....

....

Detecting Bacteria

Q1 Helen is a **Food Hygiene Manager**. She checks food hygiene practices and food safety in supermarkets. When she visits a store, she often takes **samples** of foods away for testing.

a) What **two** things will the food samples be tested for? Tick the boxes next to the correct answers.

The amount of bacteria present in the food. ☐

The presence of any harmful bacteria. ☐

The taste of the food. ☐

b) When Helen visits a supermarket, she also takes **'swabs'** from certain areas.

i) What are 'swabs'? Circle the correct answer from below.

Special cotton buds used to wipe surfaces.   Special cotton buds used to disinfect surfaces.

Antiseptic wipes.

ii) Complete the passage about **taking swabs** using some of the words below.

equipment	clean	cooked	lab	new	contaminate	chilled

In food production everything that food might come into contact with must be

.... This includes .... as

well as work surfaces. Regular checks are carried out to ensure nothing harmful

is lurking around which might .... the food during

preparation. Samples are taken using swabs. The swabs will then be taken to a

.... to be tested.

Q2 Dave works in a **microbiology laboratory**. He tests samples sent to him to find out about the microorganisms they contain.

a) Dave uses **aseptic techniques** in his work.
Tick the box next to the sentence below that explains why Dave uses these techniques.

☐ **To prevent contamination of samples during testing.**

☐ **To ensure all microorganisms are destroyed.**

☐ **To protect Dave from cuts and bruises.**

RIP

b) Briefly describe **one** aseptic technique Dave might use in his work.

....

Detecting Bacteria

Q3 Carmel works as a **water quality tester**. She has been asked to test a sample of **bottled mineral water** to find out how many microorganisms it contains.

a) i) Write numbers (1-4) in the boxes to put the sentences into the right order to show how Carmel should test the water. The first one has been done for you.

☐ Incubate the agar plate.

☐ Count the number of colonies.

☐ Spread a small amount of the sample over an agar plate.

1 Dilute the sample several times.

ii) What is this method of testing called? Circle the correct answer from the options below.

| Serial dilution | Aseptic plates | Streak dilution | Bacterial counting |

iii) Why is the original sample diluted several times? Circle the correct answer.

There are too many bacteria to count in the original sample.

Bacteria swell in water making them easier to count.

You can only see the bacteria if they are wet.

Remember, bacteria multiply very quickly.

b) After incubation, the agar plate looks like this:

— Agar plate

— Colony

i) How many **bacterial colonies** are on the plate? ....

ii) Carmel diluted her original sample (**A**) by a **factor of 10**, **three times**.

Approximately how many bacteria were in the original undiluted sample?

A   B   C   D

....

....

....

Top Tips: Remember, the number of colonies on the plate is how many bacteria were added to the plate. If you know how many times the sample was diluted and by how much, you can work out how many bacteria were in the original undiluted sample. Tricky but handy.

Section 4 — Microorganisms and Food Production

Detecting Bacteria

Q4 Ankit is a **microbiologist**. Part of his job is to grow the microorganisms found in food so they can be **identified**.

a) The diagrams below show the **method** Ankit uses to grow microorganisms.
Draw lines to match each diagram to the correct description of what is happening.

Diagram A

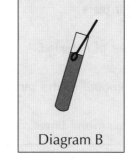

Diagram B

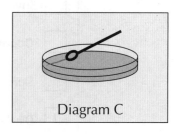

Diagram C

Spread the sample over an agar plate.

Flame a wire inoculating loop.

Dip the wire into the sample.

b) i) What is the purpose of the step shown in **Diagram A**? Circle the correct answer.

It makes the microorganisms being grown more active.

It heats up the sample.

It will get rid of any bacteria on the wire loop.

ii) Why is it important to perform the step shown in **Diagram C** and then replace the lid on the agar plate as quickly as possible? Tick the box next to the correct answer.

☐ To keep the contents of the agar plate warm.

☐ To stop too much oxygen getting in.

☐ To reduce the amount of bacteria entering the agar plate.

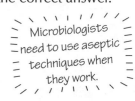

Microbiologists need to use aseptic techniques when they work.

c) Where should the agar plate be **stored** while the microorganisms are growing?
Circle the correct answer.

In the dark.   Somewhere warm.   In the fridge.

d) What piece of **equipment** will Ankit use to help him identify the microorganisms he grows?

....

e) Ankit finds evidence of **harmful bacteria** in a food sample he tests. When he **repeats the test**, he finds no evidence of the bacteria. Why does Ankit repeat the test?

....

Microorganisms in Food

Q1 Chris works for a **cheese making company**. People often ask Chris to **explain** the cheese making process. Complete his explanation using words from the box.

taste	whey	bacteria	moulds	lactose	warm	curdles

A culture of bacteria is added to .... milk. The bacteria convert

.... (the sugar in milk) to lactic acid. This .... the milk,

producing solid curds. The curds are separated from the liquid ....

More .... are added to the curds, and the whole lot is left to ripen

for a while. .... are added to give blue cheese (e.g. Stilton) its colour

and ....

Q2 **Yogtastic** is a yoghurt manufacturer. The owners think that putting an **explanation** of how yoghurt is made on their website might encourage people to buy their products **online**.

a) Number the boxes (1-5) to put the following sentences in order to describe how yoghurt is made.

- ☐ The milk is pasteurised.
- ☐ A starter culture of bacteria is added to the milk.
- ☐ All the equipment is sterilised.
- ☐ The mixture is incubated.
- ☐ The milk is cooled.

b) Draw lines to match up the words below with their correct description.

Sterilisation   Heating to 72 °C to kill off unwanted microorganisms.

Pasteurisation   Heating to 40 °C to help bacteria to grow.

Incubation   A process used to kill any microorganisms on equipment.

c) During incubation, the bacteria convert lactose sugar in the milk into lactic acid. What is this **process** called? Circle the correct answer.

respiration   fermentation   incubation

Top Tips: Microorganisms can make foods tasty. But remember, you've still got to watch out for the bad bacteria. That's why making milk and cheese involves sterilisation and pasteurisation.

Microorganisms in Food

Q3   **Froggart's Bakery** makes world famous bread. Their bread contains lots of **small holes** that make it light in texture. Grania studies **yeast** to see how she can improve the bread making process.

a)   Circle the correct word(s) in each pair to complete the following passage about yeast.

> Yeast is a type of **fungus** / **bacteria**. It converts sugar into **oxygen** / **carbon dioxide**
>
> and **lactic acid** / **ethanol**. This process is called **fermentation** / **incubation**.

b)   What makes Froggart's bread rise? Circle the correct answer.

      oxygen   carbon dioxide   lactic acid   ethanol

Q4   Clara is given a home **wine making** set as a gift. It contains a **demijohn** (a large glass container), an **air lock**, a tin of **grape juice** concentrate and a sachet of **brewer's yeast**.

a)   Put the following sentences (A-E) into the correct order to describe how Clara will make her wine.

     A Fermentation slows down as the increasing alcohol concentration kills the yeast.

     B Grape juice concentrate, warm water and yeast are added into the demijohn.

     C The demijohn is sealed and put in a warm place.

     D The yeast ferments the sugars in the grape juice into alcohol.

     E The wine is ready for bottling.

     Order — ....

b)   The airlock stops air entering the demijohn, but allows gases to escape.
   Why is it important to stop air entering the demijohn? Circle the correct answer.

       To stop unwanted   To stop the   To make sure that there
        microorganisms   demijohn from   are no gases of any sort
          getting in.   getting too full.   in the demijohn.

c)   After successfully brewing wine, Clara decides to try **beer making**.
   The process is very similar, but uses a different sugar source.

     i) What will she have to use instead of the grape juice?

     ....

     ii) What type of sugar does this contain?

     ....

Top Tips: Mmmm... bread... Don't get your yoghurt and beer making mixed up — it would taste terrible. **Yeast** is for bread, beer and wine. **Bacteria** are used for dairy — cheese and yoghurt.

Section 4 — Microorganisms and Food Production

Mixed Questions for Section 4

Q1 Red Windsor is a type of **cheese** made using **pasteurised** cows' milk.
It is blended with red wine to give it a marbled appearance.

a) Draw lines to match the type of **microorganism** with their role in food production.

Bacteria

Added to milk to make cheese

Fungus

Added to grape juice to make wine

Yeast is a type of fungus.

b) How is the milk is pasteurised? Tick the box next to the correct answer.

☐ Heating to 72 °C for 15 seconds

☐ Heating to 40 °C for 30 minutes

☐ Heating to 132 °C for one minute

Q2 The recipe below describes how you can make fresh **yoghurt** at home.

a) Why is yoghurt stored in the **fridge**?
Circle the correct answer.

It kills all of the unwanted bacteria.

It stops the bacteria from being able to grow and multiply.

It slows down the growth of bacteria.

Recipe for Home Made Yoghurt

Ingredients:
1 pint milk, 1 tbsp live plain yoghurt

Instructions:
1. Boil the milk in a large pan.
2. Cover the pan and leave it to cool to about 40°C (gently warm to the touch).
3. Mix in the live yoghurt.
4. Pour the mixture into a warm bowl, cover it and place somewhere warm for 4 hours.
5. Allow the mixture to cool and store it in the fridge.
6. Eat within 5 days.

b) Tick the correct boxes to show if the following statements are **true** or **false**.

	True	False
i) Before you start, you should sterilise all the equipment you are using.	☐	☐
ii) The milk is left in a warm place for four hours to allow bacteria from the air to get into it.	☐	☐
iii) The live yoghurt contains fungi, which is needed to turn the milk into yoghurt.	☐	☐
iv) Covering the yoghurt during cooling reduces the chance of contamination.	☐	☐
v) Fermentation of the milk produces maltose.	☐	☐
vi) Lactic acid causes the milk to clot and solidify.	☐	☐

Mixed Questions for Section 4

Q3 Liz is a **public health inspector** investigating the source of 32 cases of **food poisoning**. The victims all became infected with the *Campylobacter* **bacteria** after eating chicken at a wedding party. *Campylobacter* are present in raw chicken, but are not usually found in cooked chicken.

a) Why are *Campylobacter* not usually found in **cooked** chicken?
Tick the box next to the correct answer.

☐ *Campylobacter* is only found in eggs. ☐ Cooked chicken can only contain *E. Coli*.

☐ Cooking food properly kills *Campylobacter*. ☐ *Campylobacter* can't survive above 2 °C.

b) Suggest **one** reason why the cooked chicken may have contained *Campylobacter*.

....

c) Circle the correct word in each pair to complete the sentences below.

The serial dilution method is used to **identify / count** bacteria.

Streak plates and microscopes are used to **identify / count** bacteria.

d) During her investigation Liz visits the caterer who prepared the chicken for the wedding party. She finds that the caterer stores raw chicken in open containers in the same fridge as cooked chicken. Liz takes swabs of the fridge and sends them off for testing.

i) What substance should be used to **clean** the contaminated fridges?
Circle the correct answer.

Detergent   **Disinfectant**

ii) Why should Liz use **aseptic techniques** when collecting the swabs from the fridge?

....

....

e) Liz produces the following agar plate when testing the samples:

Agar plate

Colony

Liz diluted the original sample by a factor of 10, **five** times. Approximately how many bacteria were in the original undiluted sample?

....

....

Top Tips: If you're asked in the exam to estimate how many bacteria were in an original bacteria sample, don't panic. Yes, you've got to do a bit of maths, but you'll be told how much the original sample was diluted by, so you'll have all the information you need to work out the answer.

Section 4 — Microorganisms and Food Production

Essential Nutrients

Q1 Plants need **minerals** to grow. There are **four** main minerals that plants need.

a) Draw lines to match the minerals below with the reasons why plants need them.

Nitrates

Phosphates

Potassium

Magnesium

For a high fruit yield

For photosynthesis

For good root development

For healthy leaf growth

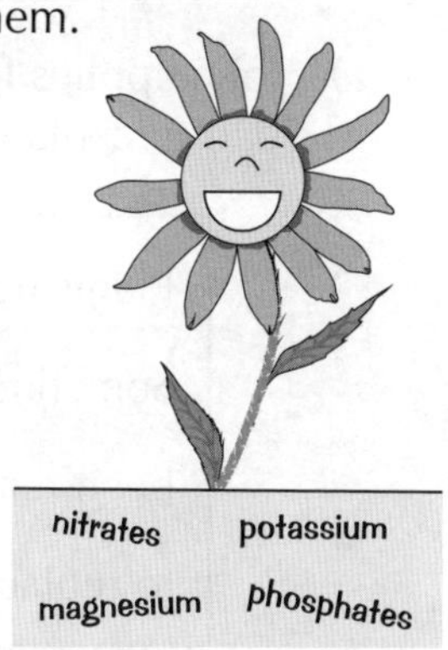

nitrates   potassium

magnesium   phosphates

b) Where do plants get minerals from? Circle the correct answer.

The air   Photosynthesis   The soil   Insects   The Sun

Q2 Joe is a **farmer** who grows wheat. He adds **fertiliser** to his fields once a year. The graph below shows the **mineral content** of the soil in one of his fields over a year.

a) Explain why the mineral content of the soil decreases between points **A** and **B**.

....

....

....

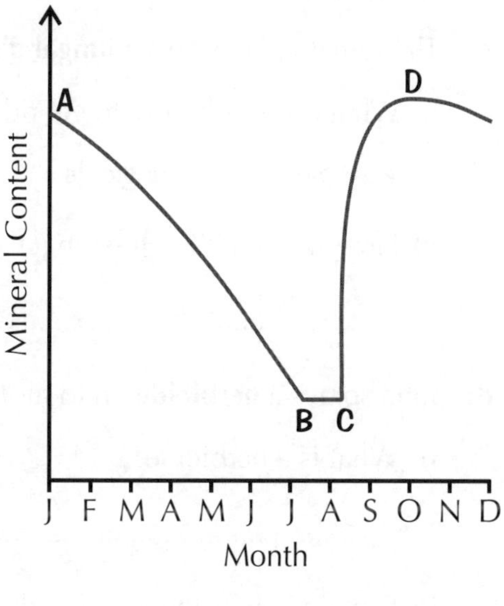

b) Why does Joe add **fertiliser** to the soil?

....

....

c) In which **month** did Joe add fertiliser to the soil? Explain your answer.

....

....

d) Joe has three different fertilisers to choose from. For each of the fertilisers below, decide whether they are a natural fertiliser or a chemical fertiliser. Circle the correct answer.

i) Manure   natural / chemical

ii) Ammonium nitrate   natural / chemical

iii) Compost   natural / chemical

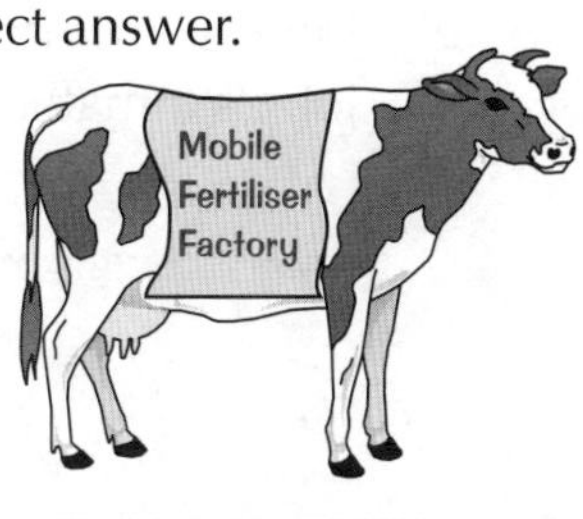

Mobile Fertiliser Factory

Intensive Farming

Q1 John manages **tomato production** on a large intensive farm.
His job involves ensuring that as **large** a crop as possible is obtained.

a) John applies **fertilisers** to the tomato plants. Circle the correct word(s) in each
pair to explain how this will affect his crop yield.

> Plants need certain minerals to **help them grow** / **make them easier to harvest**.
>
> Sometimes, the concentration of these minerals in the soil is low because they've
>
> been removed by **animals** / **other crops**. Intensive farmers use **natural** / **artificial** fertilisers
>
> to replace these elements, and this helps to **increase** / **decrease** the crop yield.

b) John's tomato plants become infested with **flea beetles** — a beetle that eats the plant.

i) What could John use to kill the beetles? Tick the box next to the correct answer.

Fungicides ☐   Pesticides ☐   Fertilisers ☐

uh-oh

ii) How would killing the beetles increase the yield of tomatoes?

....

....

c) The tomato plants gets a **fungal disease** called leaf spot, which destroys the leaves of the plant.

i) What could John use to get rid of the fungus? Circle the correct answer.

Pesticide   **Fungicide**   **Fertiliser**   **Insecticide**   **Herbicide**

ii) How would killing the fungus increase the yield of tomatoes?

....

d) John sprays a **herbicide** on to his tomato plants.

i) What is a herbicide?

....

ii) Explain how using a herbicide will increase the yield of tomatoes.

....

....

e) Improvements in how fruit and vegetables are **stored** and **transported** mean that
John's tomatoes can now be kept fresh for much longer. Explain why this is important.

....

....

More on Intensive Farming

Q1 Jamal is trying to save money on his shopping bill. He notices the **cheapest eggs** in his supermarket are labelled 'From Battery Farmed Hens'.

The passage below explains why eggs from battery farmed hens are cheaper than other eggs. Complete the passage by circling the correct word in each pair.

> In a battery farm, the hens are kept **outdoors / indoors** in **small / large** pens so they are
>
> **cold / warm** and **can / can't** move about. This means the hens use up **more / less** energy,
>
> so they will grow **faster / slower** on less food. As a result, the production costs for the
>
> farmer **increase / decrease**, which means the eggs are cheaper for the consumer.

Q2 Nina has inherited a pig farm from her grandfather. The farm has **80 pig pens**, and each pen is **100 m²**. At the moment **20 pigs** are kept in each pen. Nina researches pig farming methods, and she finds some guidelines that say that every pig needs at least **1 m²** of space.

a) What is the **maximum** number of pigs Nina could keep in each pen?

....

b) Nina makes a profit of **£2 for each pig** she sends to be slaughtered.

  i) How much **profit** would she make at the moment if she sent all her pigs to be slaughtered?

....

....

....

Work out how many pigs Nina has and then multiply it by the profit she makes per pig.

  ii) How many pigs would Nina have if she kept **50** pigs in each pen?

....

  iii) How much **more profit** would Nina make if she kept **50** pigs in each pen?

....

....

c) Nina wants to make sure her pigs stay healthy. Which of the following will **not** help to keep her pigs healthy? Tick the box next to the correct answer.

Ensuring the pigs have a good food supply. ☐   Giving the pigs enough ventilation. ☐

Keeping the pigs in small cages. ☐   Making sure the pigs have plenty of light. ☐

More on Intensive Farming

Q3   Dominic is an **agricultural consultant** who advises farmers on how to increase crop yield.
He says that sunlight is very important because plants produce their own '**food**' using **sunlight**.

a)   What is the name of the process that plants use to produce their own food?

....

b)   Write a word equation for this process.

....

Q4   Richard grows houseplants **commercially** for sale to garden centres. Over the years
Richard has spent a lot of money building **glasshouses** in which to grow his plants.

a)   Richard **burns fuel** in his glasshouses. This helps to keep the plants warm,
but there is also another benefit.

   i)   In addition to heat, what does burning fuel produce? Circle the correct answer.

   Oxygen   Herbicides   Glucose   Insecticides   Carbon dioxide

   ii) Why does this other product help Richard's plants to grow faster?

....

....

b)   Richard's glasshouses also have **artificial lighting**.

   i)   When would Richard use the artificial lighting? Tick the box next to the correct answer.

   All the time   ☐   When it's cold   ☐

   When it's dark   ☐   When it's humid   ☐

   Artificial lighting costs money, so you should use it as little as possible.

   ii) What benefit does the artificial lighting provide?

....

....

Top Tips: Gardeners (and farmers) use glasshouses because they can create ideal conditions
for plant growth, helping them maximise their profits. Make sure you know how gardeners artificially
provide plants with light, carbon dioxide and heat and how this helps to increase plant growth.

Section 5 — Farming Methods and Food Production

Organic Farming

Q1 Carlos works for the **Soil Association** — an organisation that certifies farms as organic.
His job is to check that **organic farms** are using the correct farming **methods**.

Complete the paragraph about how organic fruit and vegetables are grown using words from the box.

natural	artificial	farmed	environment

Organic fruits and vegetables are .... organically. This

means they are grown without the use of .... herbicides

and pesticides. Organic farms use .... alternatives to these

chemicals, which may be better for the ....

Q2 Ella grows her own fruit and vegetables using **organic farming methods**.

a) Suggest one substance that Ella could use as a fertiliser.

....

b) Ella removes **weeds** that compete with her crops by hand.
Give one **advantage** and one **disadvantage** of using this method.

Advantage: ....

Disadvantage: ....

c) Suggest one way Ella could destroy **pests** on her crops.

....

Q3 Isaac has made a decision to eat only **organic meat** because the animals are
kept under more **natural conditions** than when they are intensively farmed.

Which of the following statements apply to organically farmed animals?
Circle the correct answer(s).

The animals are only fed on organic foods.	The animals are kept in small pens to stop them wasting energy.	The animals' food often contains artificial chemicals.	The animals are able to roam freely outdoors.

Top Tips: Organic farming is a traditional and more natural method of farming than
intensive farming. But that doesn't mean to say it's better — both methods have their pros and cons.

Comparing Farming Methods

Q1   Susan is deciding whether to farm using **intensive** or **organic** methods.
She draws a table to compare their **features** to help her decide.

Complete Susan's table by circling the correct word in each of the boxes.
The first row has been done for you.

	Intensive Farming	Organic Farming
Amount of food produced per acre	less / ⟨more⟩	⟨less⟩ / more
Number of workers needed	less / more	less / more
Cost of food produced	less / more	less / more
Environmental damage	less / more	less / more

Q2   Ghassan works for the **Environment Agency**. He is concerned
that a local **intensive farm** is causing **environmental problems**.

a)   Draw lines to match up the methods used in intensive farming below with the
environmental problems they can cause. The first one has been done for you.

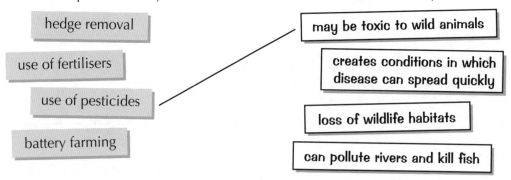

hedge removal

use of fertilisers

use of pesticides

battery farming

may be toxic to wild animals

creates conditions in which
disease can spread quickly

loss of wildlife habitats

can pollute rivers and kill fish

b)   Suggest **one** reason why hedges are often removed on intensive farms.

....

Q3   An **organic farm** is being built in a remote area of Scotland. Many local
people have complained, saying it could be bad for **wildlife** in the area.

a)   Explain how the new organic farm could be bad for wildlife.

....

....

b)   Suggest **one** way in which the organic farm could be good for the local people.

....

....

Comparing Farming Methods

Q4   Nadia is an **agricultural scientist** investigating factors that affect the **growth** of **tomato plants**.

a)   Nadia grows three different tomato plants under three different **light intensities**.

    i)   Name **two** things Nadia should keep the same during the experiment.

       1. ....

       2. ....

    ii)   Suggest **one** way Nadia could measure the growth of the plants.

       ....

b)   Nadia does a second experiment to see which of three **fertilisers** increases tomato growth the most. She grows four different tomato plants and gets these results:

	No fertiliser	Fertiliser A	Fertiliser B	Fertiliser C
Change in height of plant in 6 weeks (cm)	7	8	12	11

    i)   Complete the bar chart of her results below by drawing the two missing bars.

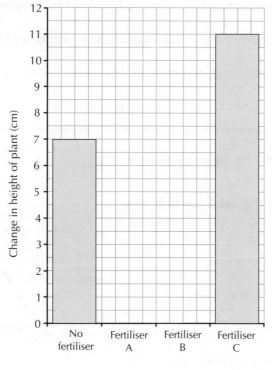

    ii)   Which is the best fertiliser used in the experiment? How can you tell?

Think about whether adding fertilisers would increase or decrease plant growth.

       ....

       ....

Selective Breeding and Genetic Engineering

Q1 Sarah has just inherited a **dairy farm**. She decides to use **selective breeding** to try and increase her profits.

a) Number the sentences below to show the stages of selective breeding in the correct order. The first one has been done for you.

[ ] Breed them with each other.

[ ] Select the best offspring.

[ ] Continue the process over many generations.

[ ] Breed them again.

[1] Select individuals with the best characteristics.

Ruminant Romance

Find the bull of your dreams *I can be quite a picky cow* *of the week: Daisy*

b) A local farmer has offered Sarah a choice of bulls to **breed** with her cows. Circle **two** characteristics that Sarah should look for in the bulls.

Good disease resistance   High milk yield in the bull's mother   Bad-tempered   Low fertility

c) The sentences below explain one of the main disadvantages of selective breeding. Complete the sentences by circling the correct word(s) in each pair.

> The main drawback of selective breeding is **a reduced / an increased** gene pool.
>
> This is where the variation in a population **decreases / increases** because the
>
> farmer keeps breeding from the best animals. As a result, if a new disease
>
> appears, **few / all** of the animals are likely to be affected.

d) The graph shows the milk yield for Sarah's cows over the last three generations.

From the graph, do you think that **selective breeding** has had an effect on Sarah's cows? Explain your answer.

....

....

....

Key: Generation 1 ———
Generation 2 ··········
Generation 3 – – – –

Number of cows (90, 80, 70, 60, 50, 40, 30, 20, 10, 0)

Milk yield / litres produced per year per cow (4000, 4500, 5000, 5500, 6000, 6500, 7000)

e) What is the **increase** in the average milk yield per cow from generation 1 to generation 3?

....

Top Tips: Selective breeding could well crop up in the exam, so make sure you know the steps — choose your best animals, breed them, choose the best offspring, breed them again and repeat. Maybe you could turn this into some kind of ritual chant... whatever gets you to learn it...

Selective Breeding and Genetic Engineering

Q2 Agricultural scientists can use **genetic engineering** to produce organisms with **desirable characteristics**. Tick the boxes to show whether the following statements about genetic engineering are **true** or **false**.

	True	False
a) Genetic engineering is the transfer of genes from one organism to another.	☐	☐
b) Genetic engineering has to be done at a late stage of development.	☐	☐
c) Genetic engineering is only possible in plants.	☐	☐
d) Genetic engineering is a more efficient way of producing organisms with desirable characteristics than selective breeding.	☐	☐

Q3 Heather is a member of a group that campaigns **against** genetically engineered foods.

a) Suggest **two** reasons why Heather might be worried about the effects of genetic engineering.

1. ....

2. ....

b) Tick **two** advantages of genetic engineering.

☐ Genetic engineering is risk free.

☐ Crops could be produced with added vitamins.

☐ Crops could be produced to be more susceptible to disease.

☐ Animals could be produced that would grow more quickly.

c) The world's population size is rapidly increasing and we need to produce more food. How could genetic engineering help with this?

....

....

Q4 Below are some statements that different people have made about **genetically modified (GM) plants**. In each case, say whether they are making an argument **for** or **against** GM technology.

a) *"Genes newly inserted into crop plants, for example for pest-resistance, may spread to nearby wild plants."* — Gregory Greene, conservationist. ....

b) **"Investing in improving traditional agricultural methods will improve yields more than investment in GM technology." — Abigail Singh, relief worker.** ....

c) *"We can produce rice plants containing toxins that are harmful to locusts but not to people."* — Veronica Speedwell, biotechnology consultant. ....

d) **"By using herbicide-resistant crops on my land, I can kill all the weeds in my field with a single dose of all-purpose herbicide**." — Ed Jones, farmer. ....

Making Chemicals for Farming

Q1 Artificial fertilisers, pesticides, insecticides and herbicides are all made using chemical reactions. These reactions are carefully controlled to make sure the chemicals can be produced **cheaply**.

Do the following things need to be **minimised** or **maximised** to ensure that the product is economical? Circle the correct answer.

Cost of the materials   minimised / maximised   Energy costs   minimised / maximised

Amount of waste   **minimised / maximised**   Yield of the reaction   **minimised / maximised**

Q2 James wanted to produce some **ammonium nitrate** to use as a fertiliser. To do this he reacted some **ammonia** with some **nitric acid**.

a) Tick the boxes below to show whether the following statements about ammonium nitrate are true or false.

                                               True   False

i) Ammonium nitrate is insoluble. ☐ ☐

ii) Ammonium nitrate is used as a fertiliser because it contains oxygen. ☐ ☐

iii) The reaction used to make ammonium nitrate is a neutralisation reaction. ☐ ☐

b) James wants to calculate the percentage yield of his reaction. To do this he will need to know the **actual yield** and the **theoretical yield** of his reaction.

i) Define the terms **actual yield** and **theoretical yield**.

Actual yield: ....

Theoretical yield: ....

ii) James calculated that he should get 2.7 g of ammonium nitrate but he actually only got 1.2 g. What was his **percentage yield**?

$$\% \text{ yield} = \frac{\text{actual yield}}{\text{theoretical yield}} \times 100$$

....

Q3 A company is producing some chemicals for farming.

Complete the table of results showing the **percentage yields** of some of their experiments.

You can use the space below for working.

Actual yield	Theoretical yield	Percentage yield
3.4 g	4.0 g	**a)**
6.4 g	7.2 g	**b)**
3.6 g	**c)**	80%
d)	6.5 g	90%

Section 5 — Farming Methods and Food Production

Controlling Chemical Reactions

Q1 Why do we usually use **catalysts**? Circle the correct letter.

A To stop reactions   B To speed up reactions

C To slow down reactions   D To make reactions reversible

Q2 Draw lines to match up the changes with their effects on the particles in a reaction.

increasing the temperature

makes the particles move faster, so they collide more often

decreasing the concentration

means more of a solid reactant will be able to react with the other reactant

increasing the surface area

means fewer particles of reactants are present in a given volume, so they'll collide less often

Q3 Below are two diagrams showing particles in boxes.

a) Which diagram could show:

i) the solution higher in concentration?

....

ii) the mixture of gases at a lower pressure?

....

A   B

b) If you increase the pressure of a reaction between two gases, does the rate of the reaction **increase** or **decrease**?

....

c) Explain your answer to part **b)**.

....

Q4 Here are four statements about **surface area** and rates of reaction.
Circle the correct word or phrase from each pair.

a) Breaking a solid into smaller pieces **increases** / **decreases** its surface area.

b) A larger surface area will mean a **slower** / **faster** rate of reaction.

c) A **larger** / **smaller** surface area decreases the number of collisions.

d) Powdered marble has a **larger** / **smaller** surface area than the same mass of marble chips.

Controlling Chemical Reactions

Q5 Choose words from the list below to complete the paragraph.

| speeding up | faster | energy | increases |

When a reacting mixture is heated, the particles move ....

This .... how often they collide. It also gives the particles more

.... All this leads to the reaction ....

Q6 Tick the correct box to show whether the statements about catalysts below are **true** or **false**.

True False

a) Catalysts are used up during a reaction. ☐ ☐

b) Only a small amount of catalyst is needed to affect the rate of a reaction. ☐ ☐

c) A catalyst will only work for a particular reaction. ☐ ☐

Q7 Circle the correct words to complete the sentences below.

Increasing your concentration will increase your rate of revision.

a) In order for a reaction to occur, the particles must **remain still / collide**.

b) If you make a solution more concentrated it means there are **more / less** reactant particles in the same volume.

c) This means that the reactant particles are **more / less** likely to collide with each other.

d) So, increasing the concentration **increases / decreases** the rate of reaction.

Q8 Haden is doing a chemical reaction. He wants the reaction to go as **quickly** as possible.

Which of the following would **increase** the rate of Haden's reaction?
Tick the boxes next to the correct answers.

Heating the reaction up. ☐   Cooling the reaction down. ☐

Using more concentrated reactants. ☐   Using less concentrated reactants. ☐

Breaking the reactants into smaller pieces. ☐   Using larger lumps of reactant. ☐

Removing the catalyst. ☐   Adding a catalyst. ☐

Top Tips: Collision theory is all about reactants bumping into each other. Anything that makes reactants bump into each other more often will increase the rate of the reaction.

Section 5 — Farming Methods and Food Production

Reversible Reactions and Ammonia Production

Q1   Look at this diagram of a **reversible reaction**.

    a)   For the forward reaction:

        i) Give the reactant(s). ....

        ii) Give the product(s). ....

    b)   Write the equation for this reversible reaction.

        ....

    c)   Name **two** things that can change the position of an equilibrium.

        ....

    d)   State whether the concentration of the reactants will be higher, lower or the same as the concentration of the products when the position of the equilibrium is:

        i) on the left. ....

        ii) on the right. ....

Q2   The Haber process is used to make **ammonia**.

    a)   Complete the equation for the reaction below.

$$........................ \ + \ .... \ \rightleftharpoons \ 2NH_{3(g)}$$

Ammonia is made from hydrogen (H_2) and nitrogen (N_2).

    b) **i)** What effect will raising the temperature have on the **yield** of ammonia?

        ....

        ii) Explain why a high temperature is used industrially.

        ....

    c)   Which of these pressures would give the **highest** yield of ammonia? Circle the correct answer.

        1000 atmospheres   **200 atmospheres**   **450 atmospheres**   **10 atmospheres**

    d)   Give **one** use of the ammonia produced via the Haber process.

        ....

Top Tips: Changing the conditions in a reversible reaction to get more product sounds great, but it's always worth considering that these conditions might be too difficult or expensive for factories to produce, or they might mean a reaction that's too slow to be profitable.

Mixed Questions for Section 5

Q1 Helen manages a **restaurant**. She is deciding whether to buy produce from **intensive** farms or **organic** farms.

a) What is intensive farming?

....

....

b) Name the type of chemical used on intensive farms to:

i) control pests ....

ii) control weeds ....

iii) control fungi ....

c) What is organic farming?

....

....

d) Helen decides to ask the restaurant customers what they think. 60% of the customers say they would pay more for meals made using organic fruits and vegetables. 80% of the customers say they would pay more for meals made using organic meat.

i) Explain why the customers would have to pay more for organic produce.

....

ii) Why do you think most of the customers would not mind paying more for organic meat?

....

Q2 Alice, an **agricultural scientist**, has been asked to find out if using a **herbicide** will increase the **yield** of carrots. She is given two small plots of land to use for her experiment. Alice plants carrots on each plot. She uses herbicide on one, but not the other.

a) Give **one** thing that Alice should keep the same on the plots.

....

b) What do you predict will happen? Tick one of the boxes below.

☐ The same mass of carrots will grow on each plot.

☐ A greater mass of carrots will grow on the plot with herbicide.

☐ A greater mass of carrots will grow on the plot without herbicide.

c) Explain your choice for question **b)**.

....

....

Section 5 — Farming Methods and Food Production

Mixed Questions for Section 5

Q3 | Sarah owns a **farm**. On the farm Sarah keeps chickens and grows aubergines.

a) Sarah wants to get as many eggs from her chickens as possible for the least amount of money.

  i) Sarah is considering using intensive farming to increase her yield of eggs. Tick the boxes to show whether the following statements about the intensive farming of chickens are true or false.

	True	False
The chickens are allowed to roam free outside.	☐	☐
The chickens are kept warm so they waste less energy giving out body heat.	☐	☐
The chickens are encouraged to move so they put on more muscle.	☐	☐
The chickens are kept in crowded conditions where disease can easily spread.	☐	☐
Intensive farming is more expensive than organic farming.	☐	☐

  ii) Sarah could also increase her yield of eggs using **selective breeding**.
Describe how Sarah could use selective breeding to increase her yield of eggs.

....

....

....

b) To increase her yield of aubergines, Sarah keeps her aubergine plants in greenhouses.
To grow effectively the aubergine plants need light, carbon dioxide and water.

  i) What process do plants use to convert light, carbon dioxide and water into food?
Circle the correct answer.

    Respiration   **Photosynthesis**   **Neutralisation**   **Eutrophication**

  ii) How could Sarah increase the amount of carbon dioxide in the greenhouses?

....

  iii) How could Sarah allow the aubergines to continue producing food after the sun goes down?

....

c) An agricultural scientist used genetic engineering to create a new strain of aubergine plants that is resistant to several common pests. Sarah agrees to try growing this strain on her farm.

  i) What is genetic engineering?

....

  ii) Because the aubergine plants are more resistant to pests, Sarah does not have to use as much pesticide on them. Explain why this could be good for the environment.

....

....

Mixed Questions for Section 5

Q4 Plants need **minerals** to grow. One of the minerals that plants need is **nitrates**.

a) i) What do plants need nitrates for? Tick the box next to the correct answer.

For photosynthesis ☐   For high fruit yields ☐

For healthy leaf growth ☐   For good root development ☐

ii) Name **three** other **minerals** that plants need to grow well.

....

b) Farmers can use **fertilisers** like **ammonium nitrate** to increase the concentration of nitrates in the soil. Ammonium nitrate is produced from ammonia and nitric acid by the reaction shown below.

Ammonia + Nitric acid → Ammonium nitrate + Water

i) What type of reaction is this? Circle the correct answer.

   Oxygenation   **Neutralisation**   **Nitrification**   **Fertilisation**   **Acidification**

ii) Ted is making some ammonium nitrate. He expected to make 65.4 g, but actually only got 52.2 g. Calculate his percentage yield.

$$\text{Percentage yield} = \frac{\text{actual yield}}{\text{theoretical yield}} \times 100$$

....

iii) Explain why using artificial fertilisers, like ammonium nitrate, can be bad for the environment.

....

....

Higher only → c) The **ammonia** (NH_3) used to make ammonium nitrate is produced from **nitrogen** (N_2) and **hydrogen** (H_2) in a reversible reaction.

i) Write a balanced chemical equation for the production of ammonia.

....

ii) How will **decreasing** the pressure affect the yield of ammonia in this reaction?

....

iii) Increasing the temperature of this reaction decreases the yield of ammonia, but high temperatures are used in industry anyway because increasing the temperature increases the rate of reaction.

Make sure you talk about particles and collisions in your answer.

Explain why **increasing** the temperature increases the rate of reaction.

....

....

....

Roles of Analytical Scientists

Q1 Below are four types of analytical scientists and some descriptions of what they do.

Draw lines to match the types of analytical scientists with the descriptions.
The first one has been done for you.

Forensic Scientist

Pharmaceutical Scientist

Environmental Scientist

Healthcare Scientist

Analyses samples to help doctors diagnose patients.

Develops and tests new drugs.

Examines substances found at crime scenes.

Collects and analyses evidence about our surroundings.

Q2 The statements below are about the work of **healthcare scientists**.

Tick the boxes to show whether the statements are **true** or **false**.

		True	False
a)	Healthcare scientists monitor air quality.	☐	☐
b)	Healthcare scientists work closely with doctors.	☐	☐
c)	Healthcare scientists analyse blood samples.	☐	☐
d)	Healthcare scientists work with businesses to reduce pollution.	☐	☐
e)	Healthcare scientists monitor the quality of drugs during manufacturing.	☐	☐

Q3 The passage below describes the role of an **environmental scientist**.

You won't need to use all of the words in the box.

Choose from the words in the box to complete the passage below.

air	laws	environment	waste	recycling
rural	food	outdoors	in hospitals	fishing

Environmental scientists work in offices, in laboratories and ....

They test and monitor .... and water quality.

They also monitor industrial .... to make sure businesses aren't breaking

any environmental protection ....

They work with industries to reduce pollution and increase ....

Many environmental scientists work for Defra (The Department for ....,

.... and .... Affairs).

Ionic Compounds

Q1   Circle the correct word(s) in each pair to complete these sentences on **ionic compounds**.

> Ionic compounds are made up of metal ions **and / or** non-metal ions.
>
> Metal ions are always **positively / negatively** charged.
>
> Non-metal ions are usually **positively / negatively** charged.
>
> Ions with **opposite charges / the same charge** are strongly attracted to each other.
>
> This gives ionic compounds a close, **regular / irregular** structure.

Q2   A **forensic scientist** is analysing a white powder taken from a suspected drug dealer. The white powder has a **high melting point** so the scientist thinks it's an **ionic compound**.

The passage below explains why ionic compounds have **high** melting points. Complete the passage using the words in the box.

energy	strong	melt	giant

Ionic compounds have a .... lattice structure consisting of

charged particles called ions. The forces of attraction between these ions are very

.... — a lot of .... is needed to overcome these

forces and .... the compound.

Q3   Some ionic compounds are **soluble** in water, but others are not. This can help analytical scientists identify ionic compounds.

Tick the boxes to show whether each of these ionic compounds is **soluble** or **insoluble**. Use the **solubility rules** on the right to help you.

	Soluble	Insoluble
a) Sodium chloride	☐	☐
b) Ammonium nitrate	☐	☐
c) Magnesium oxide	☐	☐
d) Potassium carbonate	☐	☐

Solubility Rules

- Sodium, potassium and ammonium salts are all soluble in water.
- Most chlorides are soluble in water.
- Oxides, hydroxides and carbonates are insoluble in water, except for sodium and potassium.

Formulas of Ionic Compounds

Q1 An environmental scientist was asked to analyse a sample of **industrial waste**.
The table below shows some of the **compounds** that were found in the sample.

Complete the table by filling in the formulas for each of the compounds.
The first one has been done for you.

Compound	Positive ion	Negative ion	Formula of compound
A	Ca^{2+}	O^{2-}	CaO
B	Mg^{2+}	SO_4^{2-}	
C	Na^+	CO_3^{2-}	
D	Al^{3+}	Cl^-	

Remember to make sure the charges are balanced.

Q2 The table below shows some positively and negatively charged **ions**.

Which of the **compounds** below could be formed from the ions in the table?
Circle the correct answer(s).

Positive ions	Negative ions
Sodium Na^+	Chloride Cl^-
Calcium Ca^{2+}	Sulfate SO_4^{2-}

$NaCl_2$ $CaCl_2$ Na_2SO_4 $CaSO_4$

Ca_2SO_4 $NaCl$

$NaSO_4$ $CaCl$

Q3 A red-brown solid was found at the scene of a **road accident**. It could be an **iron oxide**.

a) There are two forms of iron oxide — iron(II) oxide and iron(III) oxide.
Draw lines to match each form of iron oxide with its formula.

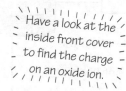

Have a look at the inside front cover to find the charge on an oxide ion.

Iron(II) Oxide   FeO

Iron(III) Oxide Fe_2O_3

b) Analysis shows that the red-brown solid contains two iron ions to every three oxide ions.
Is the compound iron(II) oxide or iron(III) oxide?

....

c) Four other metal oxides were also found at the scene. Use the list of ions below to write
the correct formulas for these compounds.

Silver — Ag^+   **Aluminium — Al^{3+}**   **Magnesium — Mg^{2+}**   **Chromium — Cr^{3+}**

i) silver(I) oxide ....   **ii)** aluminium oxide ....

iii) magnesium oxide ....   **iv)** chromium(III) oxide ....

Covalent Compounds

Q1   **Blood** and **urine** samples are often taken from murder victims to try and determine why they died. Scientists expect to find many different **organic compounds** in the samples.

a) Are the organic compounds identified likely to be **ionic** or **covalent**?

....

b) The names and formulas of some of the compounds that are commonly found in these samples are shown below. Draw lines to match each compound to its formula.

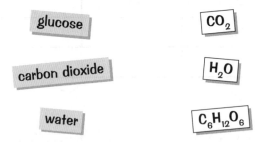

glucose CO_2

carbon dioxide H_2O

water $C_6H_{12}O_6$

c) **Ethanol** is another compound that can be found in the blood. Write the formula for ethanol.

....

Q2   When forensic scientists analyse an **unknown compound** they often measure its **melting point** and **boiling point**.

> Clive, your covalent compound has boiled over again.

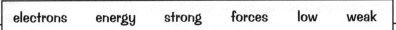

The passage below explains why the melting and boiling points of **covalent compounds** are usually **low**. Complete the passage using the words in the box.

electrons	energy	strong	forces	low	weak

Covalent compounds are usually small molecules. The atoms within the

molecules share .... Although the bonds between atoms

within a molecule are ...., the .... of

attraction between the molecules are .... Only a small

amount of .... is needed to overcome these forces, so they

melt and boil at .... temperatures.

Top Tips: Be careful not to get your compounds muddled up. Ionic compounds are made of charged particles that are strongly attracted to one another. The forces of attraction between covalent compounds tend to be weaker, which means they're often gases or liquids at room temperature.

Flame Tests and pH

Q1   **Analytical scientists** can use **flame tests** to identify metal ions.

a)   Number the sentences below so they're in the correct order to describe
how a **flame test** is carried out. The first one has been done for you.

☐   Touch the powder with the loop so that some sticks to it.

1   Dip a loop of nichrome wire in some hydrochloric acid.

☐   Rinse the loop with distilled water.

☐   Hold the loop in the blue part of a Bunsen flame.

☐   Observe and record the colour of the flame.

You have one hour to complete the test starting now.

FLAME TEST 1 HOUR

b)   Draw lines to match the **metal ions** with the **colours** of flame they would produce in a flame test.

Sodium, Na$^+$ Blue-green

Potassium, K$^+$ Lilac

Calcium, Ca^{2+} Brick-red

Copper, Cu^{2+} Orange

Q2   A **pharmaceutical scientist** is developing a new drug.
He needs to make sure that the drug has a suitable **pH**.

a)   The passage below describes how **universal indicator paper** could be used to
test the pH of the drug. Complete the passage using the words in the box.

neutral	colour	acidic	solution	alkaline

The drug is made into a .... Some of this is then dropped

onto universal indicator paper. The .... of the paper shows

the pH. Compounds with a pH less than 7 are ...., those

with a pH greater than 7 are .... and compounds with a

pH equal to 7 are ....

b)   The drug turned universal indicator paper red. Is the drug acidic, alkaline or neutral?

....

c)   Suggest another way that the pH of the drug could be tested.

....

Solubility and Carbonates

Q1 The sentences below describe how you would test the **solubility** of a compound. Complete the sentences by circling the correct word(s) in each pair.

> Add a small amount of the compound to some **distilled water / hydrochloric acid**.
>
> **Heat / shake** the boiling tube and then allow the contents to settle.
>
> If the solution becomes clear, the compound is **insoluble / soluble**.
>
> If the compound is partially soluble the solution will **turn cloudy / not change**.

Q2 For many chemical tests, a substance need to be in solution.

Put the following statements in order by writing numbers (1-4) in the boxes to describe how a solution can be made.

- ☐ Shake the boiling tube.
- ☐ Pour the solution through filter paper to remove excess solid.
- ☐ Add some solid to a boiling tube containing distilled water.
- ☐ Repeat until no more solid will dissolve.

Q3 A laboratory is testing a range of **indigestion remedies** to see if they contain the chemicals that the manufacturers say they do. One product being tested claims to contain **calcium carbonate**.

a) The apparatus below is used to test for **carbonates**. Label the diagram using the words in the box.

Carbon dioxide	Limewater	Carbonate	Acid

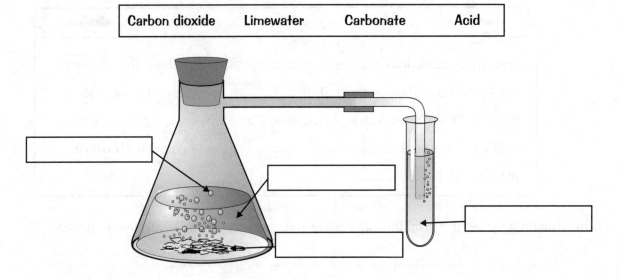

b) What will happen to the limewater if the indigestion remedy **does** contain calcium carbonate?

....

Precipitation Tests

Q1 A laboratory has been sent a sample of **polluted river water**.
They have been asked to identify the **ions** that are present.

a) Use the terms from the box to complete the passage describing how the river water
can be tested for **sulfate** and **chloride** ions. You should only use each term once.

white precipitate	nitric acid	hydrochloric acid	barium chloride	silver nitrate

To test for sulfate ions, put a sample of river water into a test tube and add some dilute

.... and then a few drops of .... solution.

If sulfate ions are present a .... will form.

To test for chloride ions, put some river water into another test tube, add some dilute

.... and a few drops of ....solution.

A white precipitate will form if there are chloride ions in the sample.

b) To identify metal ions in the river water, **sodium hydroxide solution** can be added.
Draw lines to match the ions to the colour of the precipitate that would form.

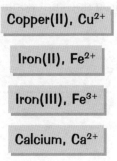   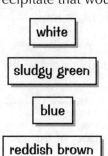   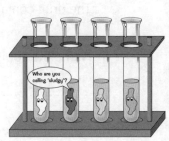

Copper(II), Cu^{2+}

Iron(II), Fe^{2+}

Iron(III), Fe^{3+}

Calcium, Ca^{2+}

white

sludgy green

blue

reddish brown

Q2 The equations for the reactions that occur during some **precipitate tests** are shown below.

a) Complete the equations using the words in the box.

sodium sulfate	silver chloride	barium sulfate		calcium chloride
calcium hydroxide		sodium chloride	iron(II) hydroxide	iron(II) nitrate

i) iron(II) sulfate + sodium hydroxide → .... + ...

ii) calcium sulfate + barium chloride → .... + ...

iii) iron(II) chloride + silver nitrate → .... + ...

iv) calcium chloride + sodium hydroxide → .... + ...

b) Circle the **precipitate** in each of the equations above.

Precipitation Tests

Q3 A pharmaceutical company says that their latest drug contains **copper sulfate**.
An analytical scientist is investigating this claim.

a) The scientist made up a solution containing the drug and added sodium hydroxide to it.

  i) What colour precipitate would form if the drug contained copper sulfate?
  Circle the correct answer.

  reddish brown   **sludgy green**   **blue**   **white**

  ii) Write a word equation for the reaction between sodium hydroxide and copper sulfate.

  ....

b) When **hydrochloric acid** and **barium chloride** were added to a solution containing the drug,
a **white precipitate** was formed.

  i) What does this tell you about the drug? Tick the box next to the correct answer.

  The drug contains calcium ions. ☐   The drug does not contain chloride ions. ☐

  The drug contains sulfate ions. ☐   The drug does not contain copper ions. ☐

  ii) Name the compound present in the white precipitate.

  ....

  iii) Name the other product of this reaction.

  ....

Q4 A powder is recovered from a suspected **bomb-making factory**.
The table shows the results of some of the tests that are carried
out on a solution of the mystery substance to try to **identify** it.

Test	Result
Sodium hydroxide added	Sludgy green precipitate forms
Dilute hydrochloric acid and barium chloride added	No change
Dilute nitric acid and silver nitrate added	White precipitate forms

a) Based on these test results, which ions were present in the compound? Circle the correct answers.

  Fe^{3+} Cu^{2+} Pb^{2+} Fe^{2+} SO_4^{2-} NO_3^- Cl^-

b) Suggest the chemical name of the mystery substance.

  ....

Testing for Ethanol

Q1   If the police suspect someone of **drink driving** they will often carry out a test at the road side. Using the words below complete the passage to describe how the **original breathalyser** worked.

| orange   potassium dichromate   ethanol   green   sulfuric acid |

The original breathalyser consisted of a tube, with a chamber containing a mixture of

potassium dichromate and ...., connected to a bag. The suspect

had to blow into the tube. If there was .... in the driver's breath it

would react with the .... causing it to change colour

from .... to ....

Q2   **Modern breathalysers** work differently to the original breathalyser.

Tick the boxes to show whether the statements about modern breathalysers are **true** or **false**.

	True	False
They give a digital read-out of the amount of alcohol in your breath.	☐	☐
They do not use acidified potassium dichromate.	☐	☐
Electronic sensors detect a colour change if ethanol is present.	☐	☐
They are still not very accurate.	☐	☐

Q3   Forensic scientists are analysing a **clear liquid** that was found in a bottle at a crime scene.

a)   Name a solution that the scientists could use to detect the presence of ethanol in the bottle.

....

b)   Give **one** way that the scientists could improve the **accuracy** of their test results.

....

....

Think about the advances in breathalyser technology.

Top Tips: In your exam you could be asked to compare the original breathalyser with modern ones — so make sure you know what's the same and what's different about how they work. That includes what chemicals they use to detect alcohol in the breath and how they each give a reading.

Identifying a Compound

Q1   A small **tablet** was confiscated from a man. The police suspect that it is an **illegal drug**. The forensic laboratory crushed the tablet into a **powder** and carried out a series of tests to identify the substance. The results are shown in the table below.

a)   Complete the table by underlining the correct conclusion in the last column. The first one has been done for you.

Test	Observation	This means the compound...
powder is put on a loop of wire and held in a blue Bunsen flame	flame turns a brick-red colour	contains sodium contains potassium <u>contains calcium</u> contains copper
powder added to dilute hydrochloric acid and any gas produced is bubbled through limewater	powder reacts, gas produced doesn't turn limewater cloudy	contains carbonate ions doesn't contain carbonate ions
powder added to water, shaken and left to settle	cloudy liquid	is soluble is slightly soluble is insoluble
The powder is made into a solution and...		
a small amount is dropped onto universal indicator paper	paper turns blue	is alkaline is neutral is acidic
a sample is added to some hydrochloric acid and barium chloride solution	a clear solution	contains sulfate ions doesn't contain sulfate ions
a sample of the solution is added to some nitric acid and silver nitrate	a clear solution	contains chloride ions doesn't contain chloride ions

b)   The table opposite shows data for some common compounds. Using both tables, what is the most likely identity of the mystery compound?

....

Compound	Solubility	pH
Magnesium hydroxide	Slightly soluble	9
Calcium chloride	Soluble	7
Calcium hydroxide	Slightly soluble	9
Sodium hydroxide	Soluble	14

c)   When carrying out a pH test, which piece of equipment would give the more **accurate** result? Tick the box next to the correct answer.

☐ **universal indicator paper**   ☐ **pH meter**

d)   Why do the scientists **repeat** all the tests they carry out?

....

Balancing Equations

Q1 In a book, this is the description of a reaction: "**methane** (CH_4) can be burnt in **oxygen** (O_2) to make **carbon dioxide** (CO_2) and **water** (H_2O)".

a) What are the **reactants** and the **products** in this reaction?

Reactants: .... Products: ....

b) Write the **word equation** for this reaction.

....

c) Write the **balanced symbol equation** for the reaction.

....

Don't forget the oxygen ends up in both products.

Q2 Which of the following equations are **balanced** correctly?

	Correctly balanced	Incorrectly balanced
a) $H_2 + Cl_2 \rightarrow 2HCl$	☐	☐
b) $CuO + HCl \rightarrow CuCl_2 + H_2O$	☐	☐
c) $N_2 + H_2 \rightarrow NH_3$	☐	☐
d) $CuO + H_2 \rightarrow Cu + H_2O$	☐	☐
e) $CaCO_3 \rightarrow CaO + CO_2$	☐	☐
f) $CO_2 + H_2O \rightarrow H_2CO_3$	☐	☐

Balanced equations have the same number and same type of atoms on each side of the equation.

Q3 Here is the equation for the formation of carbon monoxide in a poorly ventilated gas fire. It is **not** balanced correctly.

$$C + O_2 \rightarrow CO$$

Circle the **correctly balanced** version of this equation.

$$C + O_2 \rightarrow CO_2$$
$$C + O_2 \rightarrow 2CO$$
$$2C + O_2 \rightarrow 2CO$$

Top Tips: The most important thing to remember with balancing equations is that you can't change the **little numbers** — if you do that then you'll change the substance into something completely different. Just take your time and work through everything logically.

Balancing Equations

Q4   Write out the balanced **symbol** equations for the unbalanced picture equations below.

a)   +   →

You can draw more pictures to help you balance the unbalanced equations.

....

b)   +   O O   →   Li O Li

....

c)   +   →   +   +

....

d)   Li   +   →   Li O H   +   H H

....

Q5   Add **one** number to each of these equations so that they are **correctly balanced**.

a) $CuO + HBr \rightarrow CuBr_2 + H_2O$

b) $H_2 + Br_2 \rightarrow HBr$

c) $Mg + O_2 \rightarrow 2MgO$

d) $2NaOH + H_2SO_4 \rightarrow Na_2SO_4 + H_2O$

You need to have 2 bromines and 2 hydrogens on the left-hand side.

Q6   **Balance** these equations by adding in numbers.

a) $NaOH + AlBr_3 \rightarrow NaBr + Al(OH)_3$

b) $FeCl_2 + Cl_2 \rightarrow FeCl_3$

c) $N_2 + H_2 \rightarrow NH_3$

d) $Fe + O_2 \rightarrow Fe_2O_3$

e) $NH_3 + O_2 \rightarrow NO + H_2O$

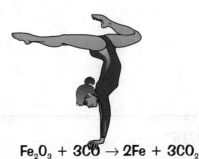

$Fe_2O_3 + 3CO \rightarrow 2Fe + 3CO_2$

Mixed Questions for Section 6

Q1 A forensic lab has been asked to confirm that a **white powder** found at a crime scene is **sodium chloride**.

a) **i)** Which of the following tests could be used to check that **sodium** is present in the sample? Circle the correct answer.

       Precipitation test   **Flame test**   **Measuring the pH**   **Solubility test**

  ii) What result would be observed if the substance contains sodium?

....

b) The white powder is made into a solution and a **silver nitrate test** is used to test for chloride ions.

  i) What would you observe when dilute nitric acid and silver nitrate are added to a solution containing sodium chloride? Circle the correct answer.

    A white precipitate   **The solution will**   **The solution will**   **Bubbles of gas will**
       will form.   **turn green.**   **turn clear.**   **be produced.**

  ii) Write a word equation for the reaction between sodium chloride and silver nitrate.

....

c) Tick the boxes to show whether the following statements about sodium chloride are **true** or **false**.

	True	False
i) It is a covalent compound.	☐	☐
ii) It contains metal ions.	☐	☐
iii) It will only melt at high temperatures.	☐	☐
iv) Its formula is NaCl.	☐	☐
v) It has a giant lattice structure.	☐	☐

Sodium ions are Na^+ and chloride ions are Cl^-.

Q2 A scientist is identifying some compounds. He does a **flame test** and measures the **pH**.

a) Complete the table to show which **metal ion** is present in each sample, and whether it's an **acid**, **alkali** or **neutral**.

Sample	Result of flame test	Metal ions present	Colour of universal indicator paper	Acid, alkali or neutral
A	Lilac		Purple	
B	Orange		Purple	
C	Lilac		Green	

b) Use the table below and the results of the lab tests to identify samples A to C.

Chemical	pH
sodium hydroxide	14
potassium hydroxide	14
potassium nitrate	7

  i) A is most likely to be ....

  ii) B is most likely to be ....

  iii) C is most likely to be ....

Section 6 — Chemical Analysis

Mixed Questions for Section 6

Q3 A forensics lab has been sent a sample of a **white powder** and asked to **identify** it to provide evidence for a police investigation. The scientists carry out a series of **tests** on the substance.

a) Some of the tests that need to be carried out are shown in the table below. Place the following sentences into the table to form a description of how each test should be carried out.

Add sample to dilute hydrochloric acid   Clean a loop of nichrome wire in hydrochloric acid

Place a drop of solution onto universal indicator paper   If solid, make the sample into a solution.

Shake and allow to settle   Collect any gas that is formed and bubble it through limewater

Place wire with sample into blue Bunsen flame

Test	Method
Solubility test	1. Add a small quantity of the sample to a boiling tube of distilled water 2.
Flame test	1. 2. Rinse with distilled water 3. Dip into sample 4.
pH test	1. 2.
Carbonate test	1. 2.

b) The non-metal ion in the compound is thought to be **sulfate**.

i) What **two** things would you add to a solution of the white powder to confirm this? Circle the correct answers.

hydrochloric acid   limewater   barium chloride

sodium hydroxide   potassium dichromate   silver nitrate

ii) What would you expect to see if sulfate ions were present?

....

c) The metal ion in the compound is thought to be **calcium**. Describe an additional test that could confirm this.

....

....

....

d) Why does the scientist carry out each test more than once? Circle the correct answer.

Performing each test more than once improves the **accuracy / reliability / speed** of the result.

Relative Formula Mass

Q1 The **relative atomic mass** of an element can be found on the periodic table.

a) The element helium is shown below as it is on the periodic table.
Circle its **relative atomic mass**.

$$^{4}_{2}\text{He}$$

b) Write down the **relative atomic masses (A$_r$)** of the following:

i) hydrogen   **ii)** oxygen   **iii)** potassium   **iv)** nitrogen   **v)** sulfur

$$^{1}_{1}\text{H} \qquad ^{16}_{8}\text{O} \qquad ^{39}_{19}\text{K} \qquad ^{14}_{7}\text{N} \qquad ^{32}_{16}\text{S}$$

....

Q2 a) Explain how the **relative formula mass** of a **compound** is calculated.

....

b) What are the **relative formula masses (M$_r$)** of the following:

Use your answers to Q1 to help you.

i) water (H_2O)

....

ii) potassium hydroxide (KOH)

....

iii) nitric acid (HNO_3)

....

iv) sulfuric acid (H_2SO_4)

....

Q3 How much will the following **weigh** in grams?

Here are some A$_r$ values you might need...
Fe = 56, Cl = 35.5, Zn = 65.

a) 1 mole of iron (Fe) ....

b) 2 moles of potassium (K) ....

c) 1 mole of hydrogen chloride (HCl) ....

d) ½ mole of zinc sulfate ($ZnSO_4$) ....

Calculating Masses in Reactions

Q1 The calculation below can be used to work out the mass of **sodium** that is needed to make **2 g** of **sodium oxide** in the following reaction: $4Na + O_2 \rightarrow 2Na_2O$

Complete the calculation by filling in the blanks.

> A_r of 4Na = 4 × .... = 92
>
> M_r of $2Na_2O$ = 2 × .... = 124
>
> 92 g of Na reacts to give 124 g of Na_2O
>
> .... g of Na reacts to give 1 g of Na_2O
>
> .... g of Na reacts to give 2 g of Na_2O

You can find all of the A_r values you'll need for these questions on the inside front cover.

Q2 Anna burns **10 g** of **magnesium** in air to produce **magnesium oxide** (MgO). The balanced equation for this reaction is: $2Mg + O_2 \rightarrow 2MgO$

a) What are the relative formula masses of:

i) 2Mg: ....   ii) 2MgO: ....

b) Calculate the mass of **magnesium oxide** that's produced when 10 g of magnesium is burnt in air.

....

....

Q3 **Aluminium** and **iron oxide** (Fe_2O_3) react together to produce **aluminium oxide** (Al_2O_3) and **iron**. The balanced equation for this reaction is: $2Al + Fe_2O_3 \rightarrow Al_2O_3 + 2Fe$

What **mass** of iron is produced from **20 g** of iron oxide?

....

....

....

Q4 When heated, **limestone** ($CaCO_3$) decomposes to form **calcium oxide** (CaO) and **carbon dioxide**.

Balanced Equation:
$$CaCO_3 \rightarrow CaO + CO_2$$

How many **kilograms** of limestone are needed to make **100 kilograms** of **calcium oxide**?

The calculation is exactly the same — just use 'kg' instead of 'g'.

....

....

....

Calculating Masses in Reactions

Q5 **Iron oxide** is reduced to **iron** inside a blast furnace using carbon. There are **three** stages involved.

> | | |
> |---|---|
> | **Stage A** | $C + O_2 \rightarrow CO_2$ |
> | **Stage B** | $CO_2 + C \rightarrow 2CO$ |
> | **Stage C** | $3CO + Fe_2O_3 \rightarrow 2Fe + 3CO_2$ |

a) If **10 g** of **carbon (C)** are used in stage B, what mass of **CO** is produced at the end of stage B?

....

....

....

b) If all the carbon monoxide produced in stage B gets used in stage C,
what **mass** of **CO$_2$** is produced at the end of **stage C**?

....

....

....

Q6 **Sodium sulfate** (Na_2SO_4) is made by reacting **sodium hydroxide** (NaOH)
with **sulfuric acid** (H_2SO_4). **Water** is also produced.

a) Write out the **balanced equation** for this reaction.

....

b) What mass of **sodium hydroxide** is needed to make **75 g** of **sodium sulfate**?

....

....

....

c) What mass of **water** is formed when **50 g** of **sulfuric acid** reacts?

....

....

....

Top Tips:
Calculation questions can be tricky, but don't worry — you're allowed a calculator in the exam which'll make things easier. Just make sure you stick in the right numbers and you're set.

Titrations

Q1   An environmental scientist is doing an **acid-base titration** to find out how much **sulfuric acid** (H_2SO_4) there is in a sample of rain water.

Talk about tight rations

a)   The passage below describes how the scientist should carry out the titration. Complete the passage using the words from the box.

colour	swirling	indicator	titration	rainwater
	neutralised		burette	

Add some of the .... to a .... flask with a

few drops of .... Fill a .... with alkali.

Add some alkali to the solution, regularly .... the flask.

Record the volume of alkali when the indicator changes ....

This happens when all of the acid in the rainwater has been ....

b)   **30 cm³** of sodium hydroxide solution (NaOH) was needed to completely neutralise the acid in **25 cm³** of the rainwater. The sodium hydroxide had a concentration of **1.5 mol per dm³**.

i)   How many **moles** of **sodium hydroxide** were used to neutralise the acid?

....   _moles = concentration × volume_

....

ii)   Use your answer to part **i)** and the balanced chemical equation below to determine how many **moles** of **sulfuric acid** were present in the rainwater.

$$H_2SO_4 + 2NaOH \rightarrow Na_2SO_4 + 2H_2O$$

....

....

iii) Use your answer to part **ii)** to work out the **concentration** of **sulfuric acid** in the rainwater.

You might need to use a formula triangle to answer this question. Have a look at the inside front cover for help.

....

....

c)   The scientist **repeated** the titration three times and calculated an **average** concentration. Why did he do this? Tick the box next to the correct answer.

☐   To make the results more accurate.

☐   To increase the reliability of the results.

☐   So he could get the results more quickly.

Titrations

Q2   An industrial company has been illegally dumping **hydrochloric acid** (HCl) in a nearby lake.

An acid-base titration showed that **15 cm³** of potassium hydroxide (KOH) with a concentration of **0.5 moles per dm³** was needed to completely neutralise the acid in a **20 cm³** sample of lakewater.

a)   How many moles of KOH are present in 15 cm³ of the 0.5 moles per dm³ solution?

....

....

b)   The balanced chemical equation for the reaction between KOH and HCl is:

$$HCl + KOH \rightarrow KCl + H_2O$$

Fill in the blanks: From the equation, ... mole(s) of HCl reacts with .... mole(s) of KOH.

c)   Use your answers to **a)** and **b)** to work out how many moles of HCl there are in 20 cm³ of lakewater.

....

....

d)   What is the concentration of HCl in the lake water in **moles per dm³**?

....

....

Q3   A scientist is using an acid-base titration to find the concentration of calcium hydroxide ($Ca(OH)_2$) in a sample. **20 cm³** of hydrochloric acid (HCl) with a concentration of **0.1 moles per dm³** was needed to neutralise all of the $Ca(OH)_2$ in **30 cm³** of the sample.

a)   Write a balanced chemical equation for the reaction between $Ca(OH)_2$ and HCl.
The products of the reaction are calcium chloride ($CaCl_2$) and water.

....

b)   Work out the concentration of $Ca(OH)_2$ in the sample.

....

....

....

....

That's it!
I've got
the solution!

Big deal.
I've got
one, too.

Chromatography

Q1   **The Environment Agency** are tracing the source of **pollution** in a river.
They use paper **chromatography** to help them analyse the pollution.

a)   Number the following statements (1-5) to show the correct method for carrying out
paper chromatography.

☐   Compare the results to reference materials.

☐   Draw a line across the bottom of a piece of filter paper.

☐   Allow time for the solvent to seep up the paper.

☐   Place spots of the samples to be tested at regular intervals along the line.

☐   Hang the sheet in a beaker of solvent.

b)   Complete the following passage using words from the list below, to describe how
paper chromatography works.

different	more	solvent	dissolve	stationary	mobile	faster	less

In paper chromatography, substances are separated by the movement of a solvent

(known as the .... phase) through a medium (known as the

.... phase). The solvent rises up the filter paper and when it

reaches the spots of sample, the chemicals in the sample ....

The solvent carries the different chemicals in the sample up the filter paper at

.... rates. The more soluble the chemical, the ....

time it spends in the mobile phase and so the .... it travels up the paper.

Q2   Gerald is trying to decide whether to use paper or thin-layer **chromatography**.

What is the main **difference** between thin-layer chromatography and paper chromatography?

....

....

Higher only

Q3   In chromatography, the **speed** that a dye moves up the medium depends on the relative
attractions of the molecules in the **dye** to the molecules in the **medium** and the **solvent**.

Draw lines to show how the rate of movement is affected by the type of attraction.

Dye molecules more strongly attracted to the medium	Dye moves slowly
Dye molecules more strongly attracted to the solvent	Dye moves quickly

Section 7 — More Analysis

Analysing Chromatograms

Q1 Ella is using **paper chromatography** to compare the **ink** used on a **threatening letter** with the ink found in three **suspects' printers**.

When Ella analyses the ink from the threatening letter and the ink from the suspects' printers she obtains the chromatogram shown on the right.

a) Suggest which ink could have been used to produce the letter.

....

b) Explain your answer to part **a)**.

....

....

Ink on letter | Ink from suspect 1 | Ink from suspect 2 | Ink from suspect 3

Q2 A scientist at the **Food Standards Agency** is testing some foods for banned **food colourings** using paper chromatography. She compares the results from three fruit juices with **reference samples** for two banned food colourings.

Banned colouring A   Banned colouring B   Fruit juice 1   Fruit juice 2   Fruit juice 3

Compare the spots contained in the colourings and the juices.

Tick the boxes below to show which colouring, if any, each of the fruit juices contains.

	contains colouring A	contains colouring B	contains neither
Fruit juice 1	☐	☐	☐
Fruit juice 2	☐	☐	☐
Fruit juice 3	☐	☐	☐

Top Tips: Chromatography can be used to compare all sorts of things — inks, colourings, chemical mixtures... the list goes on. You could be asked a question about any of these in the exam. The principle is always the same though. Just compare the patterns of dots and see if they match.

Analysing Chromatograms

Q3   The following questions are about the chromatogram shown below.

a)   Tick the boxes below to show whether the
following statements are **true** or **false**.

True False

i) The unknown mixture contains 1 substance.

ii) Substance A has the smallest R_f value.

iii) Substance B is in the unknown mixture.

iv) Substance C is not in the unknown mixture.

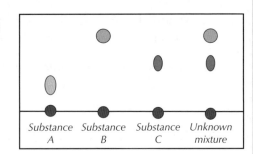

b)   If the solvent travelled 20 cm and substance A travelled 5 cm, what is the R_f value for substance A?

$$R_f = \frac{\text{distance travelled by substance}}{\text{distance travelled by solvent}}$$

....

Q4   A healthcare scientist is using
thin-layer chromatography to identify
the proteins that are present in a urine
sample from a patient.

She compares the chromatogram
of the urine sample to a chromatogram
of different protein samples. Both
chromatograms are shown on the right.

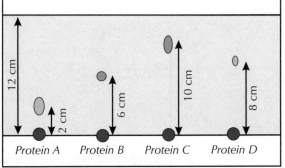

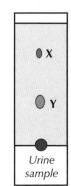

a)   Complete the table below by calculating the **R_f values** for proteins A-D.

Protein	A	B	C	D
R_f value				

b)   **Spot X** on the chromatogram of the urine sample has an R_f value of **0.68**.
Which protein is **spot X** most likely to be?

....

c)   **Spot Y** on the chromatogram of the urine sample has an R_f value of **0.32**.
What does this tell you about the protein in **spot Y**?

....

Comparison Microscopes

Q1 Lynnette is a **firearms expert**. She's using a **comparison microscope** to examine a **bullet** fired during an armed robbery and a bullet **test-fired** from a suspect's gun.

a) Complete the paragraph about comparison microscopes by circling the correct word(s) in each pair.

> Comparison microscopes are used to **compare** / **analyse** two pieces of evidence.
>
> They are made of two **electron** / **light** microscopes. When Lynnette looks into the
>
> comparison microscope she sees the two bullets **next to** / **on top of** each other.

b) Lynnette finds that the **rifling marks** on the two bullets are **identical**.

i) What are rifling marks? Circle the correct answer.

Markings which show the calibre of a bullet.

Lines on a bullet produced during the manufacturing process.

Lines on a bullet produced by imperfections in the gun barrel.

Markings on a bullet which can indicate where it was fired.

ii) Do the rifling marks prove that the gun belonging to the suspect was involved in the armed robbery? Give a reason for your answer.

....

....

c) Name **two** features of the bullets, other than rifling marks, that Lynnette might compare.

1. ....

2. ....

Q2 The police suspect a factory of dumping **toxic waste** into a river. **Forensic scientists** have collected samples of **seeds** from the river bank where the waste was dumped and some items of **clothing** from the factory workers. Some seeds are found on one of the workers' trousers.

a) Tick **three** boxes to show which features of the seeds the forensic scientists will compare.

Colour ☐   Weight ☐   Size ☐

Taste ☐   Smell ☐   Shape ☐

b) Why might the seeds be useful in this investigation?

....

....

Polarising Microscopes

Q1   Forensic scientists are using a **polarising microscope** to examine some of the evidence relating to a **murder case**.

a)   Polarising microscopes have a number of advantages. Tick the boxes next to any of the following statements that apply to polarising microscopes.

☐   They let you look at two separate slides next to each other.

☐   They reveal things that can't be seen using a light microscope.

☐   They use a beam of electrons, giving greater magnification.

b)   The scientists are analysing some **hair** samples.
Give **three** features of hair fibres that could be used to compare samples.

1. ....

2. ....

3. ....

c)   The pictures below show **three human hairs** under a polarising microscope. One of the hairs was found at the crime scene. The other two have been taken from suspects.

Hair found at crime scene   **Suspect A**   **Suspect B**

i)   Which of the hairs most closely matches the hair found at the crime scene?

....

ii) Name **one** feature that is the same.

....

d)   The scientists also use a polarising microscope to look at **soil** samples.

i)   Circle **two** features of soil that the scientists will use to compare samples.

taste   smell

                                      size of particles   colour

      water content   weight

ii) Why can soil samples be useful pieces of forensic evidence?

....

....

Top Tips: It's important to remember that things like carpet fibres or clothing fibres aren't usually unique, but they can still come in very handy when trying to link a suspect to a crime scene.

Section 7 — More Analysis

Electron Microscopes

Q1 The getaway car used in a **bank robbery** hit a **bollard** in the road as it sped away from the crime scene. Forensic scientists collected **flecks of paint** that were transferred from the vehicle to the bollard. They examined the flecks using a **light microscope** and an **electron microscope**.

a) Tick the boxes to show whether the following statements about **electron microscopes** are true or false.

True False

i) They use a beam of electrons to produce an image. ☐ ☐

ii) They produce less detailed images than light microscopes. ☐ ☐

iii) They have greater magnification than light microscopes ☐ ☐

iv) You can view the image produced by looking through the eye piece. ☐ ☐

b) The scientists analyse the flecks of paint found on the bollard and a paint sample from the getaway car. The results are shown below.

Electron micrograph of paint flecks found on the bollard.

Electron micrograph of paint from the getaway car.

Name **one** feature that the paint samples have in common.

....

c) What **three** pieces of information about the getaway car might be obtained by looking at the paint?

1. ....

2. ....

3. ....

Q2 The picture below shows an image of a **pollen grain** taken using an electron microscope. The pollen grain was found on the **clothing** of a man charged with the **burglary** of a warehouse.

a) Give **three** features of the pollen grain that forensic scientists will have used to identify it.

1. ....

2. ....

3. ....

b) The pollen found on the suspect's clothing was matched to the pollen of a plant found at the rear of the warehouse. Does this evidence provide a link between the suspect and the crime scene?

....

Instrumental Methods

Q1 Forensic scientists use **instrumental methods** to analyse substances found at crime scenes.

a) Which **one** of these is **not** an advantage of using instrumental methods over more basic lab methods? Circle the correct answer.

They are more reliable   They are cheaper   They can be automated

They are more accurate   They can detect very small amounts of substance   They are faster

b) Tick the boxes to show whether the following statements about **instrumental methods** are true or false.

	True	False
Paper chromatography, thin-layer chromatography and gas-liquid chromatography are all instrumental methods.	☐	☐
Instrumental methods use machines that must be operated by trained chemists.	☐	☐
Infrared spectrometry is an instrumental method that can only be used to identify gases.	☐	☐
Mass spectrometry is an instrumental method that can be used to work out the mass of the molecules in a substance.	☐	☐

Q2 A scientist is using **gas-liquid chromatography** to identify an unknown mixture. The chromatograms she produced are shown below.

Mixture A   Mixture B   Mixture C   Unknown Sample

a) What does each peak on a chromatogram represent?

....

b) Which mixture is the unknown sample the same as? Circle the correct answer.

Mixture A   **Mixture B**   **Mixture C**

Q3 Forensic scientists use **gas-liquid chromatography** to compare a substance found at a crime scene to a substance found on the clothing of a suspect.

Using the chromatograms on the right, is there evidence linking the suspect to the crime scene? Explain your answer.

Substance from crime scene   Substance from suspect's clothing

....

....

....

Instrumental Methods

Q4 Karl and Simon work in a forensics laboratory. Karl has been accused of stealing the last cookie from the cookie jar. Simon uses **mass spectrometry** to compare some crumbs found on Karl's sleeve to the crumbs left at the bottom of the cookie jar. His results are shown below.

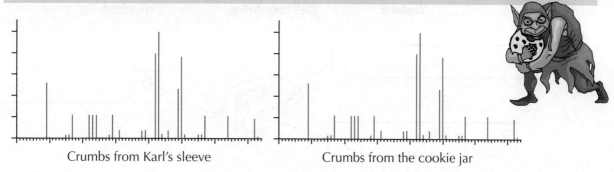

Crumbs from Karl's sleeve   Crumbs from the cookie jar

a) What name is given to the patterns of lines produced during mass spectrometry experiments? Circle the correct answer.

electron micrograph

chromatogram   titration

infrared spectrum   fragmentation pattern

b) Does the evidence from the mass spectrometry support the idea that Karl stole the last cookie from the cookie jar? Explain your answer.

....

....

Q5 A factory is suspected of having illegally dumped some toxic waste at the side of a road. **Infrared spectrometry** was used to compare a sample of the substance from the side of the road to substances found at the factory.

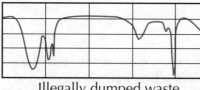

Illegally dumped waste

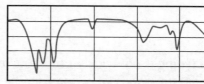

Substance A from factory

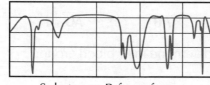

Substance B from factory

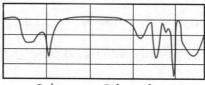

Substance C from factory

Do any of the substances found at the factory match the waste that was illegally dumped at the side of the road? Explain your answer.

....

....

Blood Group Typing

Q1 The picture below shows a type of blood cell under a **microscope**.

a) i) Label the picture using the words below.

Nucleus   Cell membrane   Cytoplasm

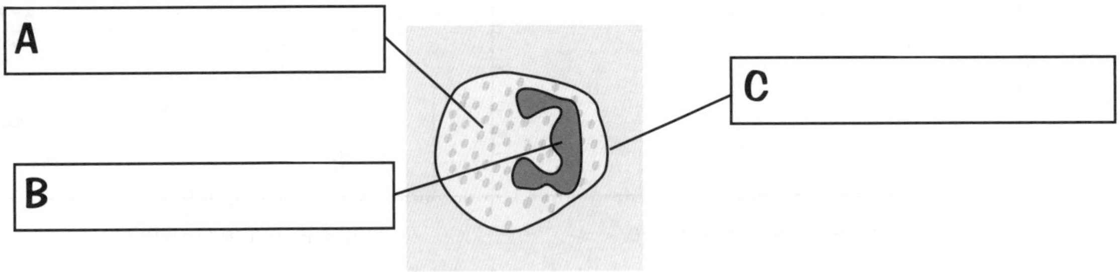

A

C

B

ii) Which part of the blood is shown in the picture above? Circle the correct answer.

Red blood cell   White blood cell   Platelet

b) Draw lines to match the components of blood with their main function.

Red blood cells

White blood cells

Platelets

Plasma

transports dissolved substances

carry oxygen

aid blood clotting

help defend the body against disease

Q2 **Blood group typing** is not widely used now in forensic science, but it used to be a common test carried out by forensic scientists to **link** a suspect to a crime.

a) Which of the following are human blood groups? Circle the correct answer(s).

O   BO   A   AB   AO   B

b) What do scientists **mix** with blood samples to determine their blood group?

....

c) Blood group typing can be used to narrow down a list of suspects but it can't be used to identify one suspect. Why is this? Tick the box next to the correct statement.

☐ Everybody has the same type of plasma.

☐ There are only four blood groups, so there are millions of people with the same blood group.

☐ You can't tell the difference between blood groups A and B by blood typing.

Blood Group Typing

Q3 Sometimes **forensic scientists** are required to give **evidence** in **court**. They have to be able to explain complex ideas such as blood group typing to ordinary members of the public.

Using words from the list below, complete the following paragraph to show how a forensic scientist might explain what blood groups are and how they are determined.

Words may be used once, more than once or not at all.

| plasma | red | platelets | antibodies | antiseptic | clot | white | antigens |

A person's blood group depends on what type of ....

are on the surface of their .... blood cells. Blood

.... can contain anti-A or anti-B ....

Scientists can test for blood group by mixing different .... with

blood samples. If anti-A .... meet A ....

(or if anti-B .... meet B ....), the blood will

....

Q4 Forensic scientists are analysing some **bloodstained clothing** from a murder suspect. Before determining the **blood group**, they first test the blood using **anti-human antibodies**.

a) Why do the scientists test the blood with anti-human antibodies before they test for blood type?

....

b) i) The scientists test for blood type by adding antibodies and observing whether clots form. Complete the table below to show what the scientists would observe for different blood types.

Blood group	Anti-A antibodies added	Anti-B antibodies added
A	Blood clots	Blood doesn't clot
B		
AB		Blood clots
O	Blood doesn't clot	

ii) The murder victim's blood group was **AB**. The blood found on the **suspect's clothing** does not clot when **anti-A antibodies** are added. Could the blood on the suspect's clothing be from the murder victim? Give a reason for your answer.

....

....

DNA Profiling

Q1   **DNA profiling** is an important tool, widely used by forensic scientists to link a suspect to a crime scene.

a)   Complete the passage about DNA profiling using words from the list below.

| unique | suspect | cousins | similar | identical twins | victim |

DNA profiling involves comparing DNA samples. It's useful because everyone's DNA is

.... (with the exception of ....).

DNA found at a crime scene can be compared to the DNA of a ....

to see whether it matches.

b)   Give **two** samples that scientists might collect from a crime scene that could contain DNA.

1. ....   2. ....

c)   The diagram on the right shows a cell from a blood sample. On the diagram, label and name the part of the cell that contains DNA.

Q2   Forensic scientists were examining a **stolen car** that had been recovered. DNA was extracted from a hair found on the headrest of the car. They created a **DNA profile** for the hair found in the car and for DNA from two suspects.

Unknown DNA from crime scene   DNA from suspect A   DNA from suspect B

a)   Does the DNA of either suspect match the DNA found at the crime scene? If so, which one?

....

b)   What does this evidence show?

....

Top Tips: DNA profiling is extremely accurate. Very occasionally two people do have the same DNA profile (especially if they're related). There are usually other things that can be used to back up DNA evidence in court though — like information about the defendant's movements or possible motive.

DNA Profiling

Q3 Kevin, Dwane and Chelsea are guests on the Jeremy Gobbard show, a popular daytime TV talk show. Chelsea claims that Kevin is the **father** of her three month old daughter Chantelle. However, Dwane claims to be the father. Kevin has asked for a **paternity test**. The results are shown below.

Chelsea   Chantelle   Kevin   Dwane

Compare the bands in Chantelle's DNA profile with those of Kevin and Dwane.

a) Does the paternity test suggest that either Kevin or Dwane is the father? If so, which one?

....

b) Why is DNA particularly useful when carrying out a paternity test? Tick the correct answer.

☐ Parents inherit DNA from their children, so their DNA profiles will be similar.

☐ A child's DNA profile will be exactly the same as their father's.

☐ Children inherit DNA from their parents, so their DNA profiles will be similar.

Q4 Sue, a forensic scientist, is analysing some **DNA** samples from a **crime scene**.

a) Put numbers in the boxes (1-5) so that the following sentences are in the correct order to describe how a DNA profile is created. The first one has been done for you.

☐ Cut the DNA into fragments.

[1] Collect evidence from the crime scene.

☐ Separate the DNA fragments using electrophoresis.

☐ Treat the DNA to make it visible.

☐ Extract the DNA from the cells.

b) When Sue carries out electrophoresis, the DNA fragments move towards the **positively charged** end of the gel. Explain why this happens.

....

....

....

c) Complete the following sentence by circling the correct word in each pair.

The **smallest** DNA fragments travel the **fastest** / **slowest** through the gel, which means they cover a **greater** / **shorter** distance.

Section 7 — More Analysis

Identifying Glass: Blocks

Q1 Different types of glass and plastic **refract** light by different amounts.

a) What is refraction?

....

....

b) Tick the boxes to show whether the following
statements about refraction are **true** or **false**.

                  True False

i) Refraction is caused by light waves changing speed.

ii) When light enters a more dense medium it is refracted towards the normal.

iii) The angle of incidence is the angle between the refracted ray and the normal.

iv) When a light ray passes from glass into air it will be refracted towards the normal.

Q2 Gideon is a trainee forensic scientist. He has been asked
to **calculate** the **refractive index** of some **glass blocks**.

a) The passage below describes how to collect the data needed to calculate
refractive index. Complete the passage using the words in the box.

To complete the passage you'll have to use some words more than once.

right angles	incidence	angle	normal	light	straight	protractor

1. Draw a .... line on a piece of paper — this is the ....

2. Place the glass block at .... to the ....

3. Shine a fine beam of .... so that it meets the block at an

   .... to the ....

4. Measure the angles of .... and refraction using a ....

b) The diagram below shows light being refracted through one of Gideon's glass blocks.
Calculate the refractive index of this glass block.

$$\text{Refractive index} = \frac{\sin i}{\sin r}$$

normal — Incident ray — 30° — 12° — Refracted ray — Emergent ray

....

....

....

....

Section 7 — More Analysis

Identifying Glass: Fragments

Q1 Gavin has been arrested by the police on suspicion of **burglary**. Forensic scientists analysing Gavin's clothes have found **shards of glass** that they can **compare** to the **window** that was broken to gain entry to the premises.

a) The scientists use the **oil immersion temperature method** to determine the refractive index of the glass found on Gavin's clothes and the refractive index of the glass from the window.

i) The first step is to mount the glass fragments on a **microscope slide** with some **silicone oil**. Complete the passage below using the words in the box.

temperature	index	clear	refractive

Silicone oil is a ...., colourless liquid.

Its .... changes with ....

ii) Once the glass is mounted, it is placed onto a **hotstage** and viewed under a **microscope**. Why is the slide placed onto a hotstage?

....

....

iii) Which part of the slide should be focussed on when it is viewed under a microscope? Circle the correct answer.

the centre of the slide　　**the centre of the glass fragment**　　**the edge of the slide**　　**the boundary between the glass fragment and the oil**

iv) Circle the correct word(s) in each pair to complete the following sentences.

> As the temperature of the oil rises, its refractive index **increases / decreases**.
>
> When the refractive index of the oil is **double / the same as** the refractive index of the
>
> glass fragment, the boundary between the glass and the oil will **crack / disappear**.

b) Gavin claims that the glass fragments came from a **milk bottle** that he dropped earlier that morning. The results of the forensic scientist's investigations are shown below.

There's no use crying over spilt milk... bottles

Refractive index of glass from window	Refractive index of glass milk bottle	Refractive index of glass from Gavin's clothing
1.569	1.474	1.474

What conclusion can be drawn from these results?

....

....

Mixed Questions for Section 7

Q1 Police are investigating a **hit and run** incident in which a pedestrian was injured by a car. **Flecks of paint** and **fragments of glass** that are likely to have come from the car involved in the incident were collected from the victim's **clothing**.

a) Forensic scientists examine the flecks of paint under a microscope.

i) What type of microscope should the scientists use? Circle the correct answer.

electron microscope   light microscope   comparison microscope   polarising microscope

ii) Give **two** features of the paint that the scientists will look at.

1. ....

2. ....

b) The police visit a local man who owns a car like the one involved in the incident. They examine the man's car and find that one headlight is broken. Forensic scientists measure the **refractive index** of the **glass fragments**.

i) Put numbers (1-6) in the boxes so that the following sentences are in the correct order to describe the method the scientists would use. The first one has been done for you.

☐ Put the slide into a hotstage.

☐ Cover the sample with silicone oil and a cover slip.

1 Place the glass sample onto a microscope slide using tweezers.

☐ Record the temperature at which the 'boundary' disappears.

☐ Put the sample under a microscope and focus on the 'boundary'.

☐ Slowly heat the oil using the hotstage.

> Estoy enfermo

A foreign sick scientist

ii) The refractive index of the glass from the car was the same as the refractive index of the glass from the victim's clothing. Does this evidence provide a link between the car and the crime scene? Explain your answer.

....

....

Higher only

c) The owner claims his car couldn't have been involved because he was away at the time of the incident. He has a receipt from a petrol station to back up his claim. Forensic scientists use **mass spectrometry** to compare the petrol in the car's fuel tank to petrol from the petrol station.

Should the police believe the man's story? Explain your answer.

....

....

....

....

Petrol from the suspect's car

Petrol from the petrol station the suspect claims to have been at

Mixed Questions for Section 7

Q2 Police are investigating the **shooting** of a young man. A **bullet** retrieved from the crime scene has been sent away for **forensic analysis**.

a) The bullet used in the shooting is compared to a bullet that was test-fired from a gun found in a suspect's possession.

The pictures on the right show the two bullets.

 Bullet from crime scene

 Bullet test-fired from the gun found in suspect's possession

   i) What feature of the bullets is enlarged in the picture? ....

   ii) Does this evidence prove that the suspect's gun was used in the shooting? Explain your answer.

   ....

   ....

b) Forensic scientists have found a **bloodstain** on clothing belonging to the suspect. The victim's blood group is A. The scientists add anti-B antibodies to a sample taken from the suspect's clothing. What result would they expect to observe if it was the victim's blood?

   ....

c) The scientists decide to use **DNA profiling** to compare the DNA from the blood found on the suspect's clothing with the DNA of the victim. The results are shown below.

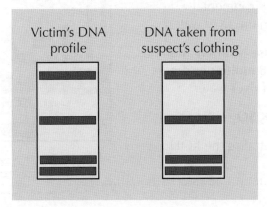
Victim's DNA profile   DNA taken from suspect's clothing

   i) Give one advantage of using DNA profiling over blood group typing.

   ....

   ....

   ii) What conclusion can be drawn from this test?

   ....

   ....

d) The victim received a threatening letter two weeks before he died. Forensic scientists used chromatography to compare the ink on the letter to ink in the suspect's printer.

   Is it likely that the suspect wrote the letter? Explain your answer.

   ....

   ....

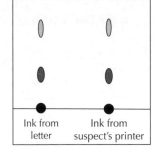
Ink from letter   Ink from suspect's printer

Top Tips: Forensic scientists would never carry out just one test — they carry out loads of different ones based on all the different evidence they find at a crime scene. That's what you've got to do here — take all the evidence, evaluate it and bring it together to draw some conclusions.

Mixed Questions for Section 7

Q3   A chemical factory makes **potassium hydroxide** (KOH) by passing an electric current through a solution of potassium chloride (KCl). The overall equation for this process is shown below.

$$2KCl + 2H_2O \rightarrow 2KOH + Cl_2 + H_2$$

Here are some A_r values you might need...
H = 1, O = 16, Cl = 35.5, K = 39.

a)   What are the relative formula masses of:

i) 2KCl: ....   **ii)** 2KOH: ....

b)   Complete the calculation below to work out what mass of KOH would be produced if **150 kg** of **KCl** were used in this reaction.

.... kg of KCl reacts to give .... kg of KOH   *Use your answers to part a) here.*

1 kg of KCl reacts to give .... kg of KOH

150 kg of KCl reacts to give .... kg of KOH

c)   What mass of KCl would be needed to produce **1000 kg** of **KOH**?

....

....

....

d)   The manager of the factory thinks that KOH could be leaking out of the factory into a nearby river. He asks an environmental scientist to measure the concentration of KOH in the river water.

The environmental scientist performs an **acid-base titration** and finds that **25 cm³** of H_2SO_4 with a concentration of **0.8 moles per dm³** is needed to neutralise all of the KOH in **50 cm³** of river water.

$$2KOH + H_2SO_4 \rightarrow K_2SO_4 + 2H_2O$$

i) How many **moles** of H_2SO_4 were used to neutralise the KOH?

Concentration = $\dfrac{moles}{volume}$

....

....

ii) Use your answer to part **i)** to work out how many **moles** of **KOH** were present in the river water.

....

....

iii) Use your answer to part **ii)** to work out the **concentration** of **KOH** in the river water.

....

....